Supertuning Your Z-28 Camaro

Supertuning Your Z-28 Camaro

by Joe Oldham

First published by Tab Books under the same title. Reprinted by Mo-
torbooks International Publishers &
Wholesalers, Inc. Osceola, Wiscon-
sin 54020 U.S.A.

1 2 3 4 5 6 7 8 9 10

Library of Congress Cataloging in Publication Data

Oldham, Joe.
   Supertuning your Z-28 Camaro.

   Includes index.
   1. Camaro automobile.   2. Automobiles, Racing.
3. Automobiles, Racing—Motors—Modification.   I. Title.
TL215.C33042   1984   629.2′504   84-980
ISBN 0-87938-184-1 (soft)

Cover photograph by Cliff Gromer

Contents

Preface

In retrospect, we were all dumb. All us so-called knowledgeable car enthusiasts were too stupid to really recognize the inherent greatness in Chevrolet's Z28 Camaro when it was first introduced. In fact, we practically ignored it.

We had our reasons. We were all horsepower and cubic-inch hungry in an era that surely had a surfeit of horsepower and cubic inches. Why should we bother with a car that had "only" 302 cubic inches and put out "only" 290 horsepower? Why should we, when roaming the streets in those days were 400-inch GTOs rated 370 horsepower, Corvettes with 454 cubic inchers rated pumping an eyeball-searing 460 horsepower, and even Buicks running around with Stage I 401s rated almost 400 horsepower?

Indeed, even other models of Camaros, the SS models could be had with 350 and 396 cubic inch engines rated up to 375 (actually 425) solid lifter horsepower. In 1969, Chevrolet even built a brace of SS Camaros with the all-aluminium ZL-1 427 engine rated at 430 horsepower.

The Z28? It was looked on as kind of an oddball. A car that was nice to drive and felt pretty good when you punched it. But no street freak would be caught dead buying one. It was more for the sporty car type who wanted to buy an American car with four seats. It certainly didn't have the balls to run with the real muscle cars of the day, so all of us knowledgeable car enthusiasts had trouble positioning it in the scheme of things. The Z28? Oh yeah. That's like Chevy's answer to the Shelby Mustang, right?

Wrong. It was more, much more, than merely answering a challenge in the marketplace. In retrospect, it was a portent of things to come. And thank heaven, the Chevrolet product planners had the foresight to think of the concept at all. A small, well-balanced sporty car that could comfortably carry four people and some luggage: powered by a small, but highly tuned, very responsive engine that not only put out terrific amounts of horsepower and torque but, because it carried around 150 less cubic inches than many of its peers, managed to get possibly 30% better gas mileage too.

Oh, if we only could have that engine now!

Over the years, the Z28 became a more and more sophisticated package—more in the mold of a European touring car than a gutsy sports car. And except for a couple of years when Chevrolet's product planners and managers did lose sight of the marketplace and dropped the Z28 altogether, the car had remained one of America's premier performance machines, out-accelerated by a very few, out-handled by no one.

The Z28 is a great car. It's a car that's recognized as something special in the world of motor cars. It's a car that makes its driver something special—one who recognizes the finer points of driving. It's a car to be proud to own and collect.

In retrospect, we should have known this would happen. At least we know it now.

Joe Oldham

7

Acknowledgements

Special thanks must go to several people for their help both directly and indirectly in the preparation of this book. First of all, to Jim Williams, director of public relations at Chevrolet. Second, to several members of his staff, especially Bruce MacDonald and Gloria Jezewski. Third, to Judy Stropus of JVS Enterprises, who not only made some of her personal photographs available to me but has also been incredibly helpful through the years in allowing me access to Chevrolet test vehicles and other material. Lastly, special thanks to the guys at Chevrolet Engineering, especially Jim Ingles, Bob Dorn, Dave McLellan and Vince Piggins, the guys who make it happen.

Chapter 1
History of The Z28

Was the original Z28 a marketing decision to sell more Camaros? Or was it a racing decision by Chevrolet? Like so many other executive decisions that take place in the automobile industry, the answer to these questions will probably be forever locked in some executive washroom on the 14th floor of the General Motors building in Detroit. There are several accounts of what actually happened, but the concensus of recall seems to weave a story something like that which follows.

THE BIRTH OF THE Z28

At the end of the 1966 racing season, Mark Donohue and Roger Penske kicked around the idea of trying one of Chevrolet's just introduced Camaros against the Mustangs in the year-old Trans Am racing series. Roger's primary interest was to promote more sales for his Chevrolet dealerships. Donohue's main interest was winning races. He had spent much time in a 1965 Mustang that had been built on a shoestring, and he had done quite well with the car. Donohue felt that he could win it all if he had a first-class car under him for the 1967 season.

The Trans Am racing series was a Sports Car Club of America series for sedans, the rules of which were governed by Group II of Appendix J of the Federation International de l'Automobile's Sporting Code. Group II sedans were supposedly production touring cars, modified only slightly—in the interests of safety—for competition. To compete in the events, the manufacturer had to produce 1000 identical cars before the FIA would certify that it was a production car. The SCCA imposed several additional restrictions, including a maximum wheelbase of 116 inches and a maximum engine displacement of 5 liters (305.1 cubic inches).

Chevrolet had no intention of entering passenger cars in sedan races. But there was such a hue and cry from road-racing Chevy lovers that management was persuaded to make a suitable vehicle available and have it certified for competition ("homologated" in the obtuse jargon of the FIA), just as Chevrolet had done with the Corvette in the sports car classes.

Actually, the Chevy II would have been a more competitive basis on which to build a Group II sedan, because it was a lighter car. But Chevrolet liked to think of the Chevy II as a family sedan and the Camaro as a sporty car, and would just as soon have had the public think likewise.

With Penske's goading, a few people at Chevrolet decided to go into action (Fig. 1-1). There was only one small hitch, however. The Camaro was available only with a 250 cubic inch, 6-cylinder engine (not powerful enough) and the 327 and 350 cubic inch V8s (over the limit). If the standard Chevy 283 cubic inch had originally been offered with the Camaro, that's probably the engine Chevy would have homologated. But starting from scratch, the opportunity to create a new engine with a displacement close to sedan racing's maximum proved tempting. And it could be easily built up from existing hardware on the Chevrolet parts department shelves.

The Z28 Engine

Chevrolet's engineers took the crankshaft from the 283 with its 3-inch stroke and put it into a 387 block with its 4-inch bore. The result was the Z28's 302 cubic inch displacement (Fig. 1-2).

The Z28's engine was special in several other respects. It had mechanical valve lifters, which are noisier than hydraulics but allow higher engine rpm. The carburetor was a high-flow capacity (800 cubic feet per minute) Holley 4-barrel sitting atop a high-rise aluminum intake manifold (also see Fig. 1-3). The intake system was fed from a plenum chamber picking up cool air from the grill near the base of the windshield, a trick invented by Chevy engineers for their 427 cubic inch Mark II racing engine in 1963 (Fig. 1-4). The Z28's heads from the high-performance 327 featured large valve—2.02 inches for the intake and 1.60 inches for the exhaust. Dual-point transistor ignition, a 5-blade discus drive fan and double fan belt pulleys were also all standard on the Z28.

Fig. 1-1. The first Z28s off the line didn't carry the Z28 identification. The '67-'68 models were virtually identical. This is a 1967.

There were some initial problems with the exhaust system on the Z28. Chevrolet engineers wanted to install fabricated steel-

Fig. 1-2. This 302 cubic inch engine pumped 290 horsepower. It was used on all Z28s from 1967 through 1969.

Fig. 1-3. Optionally available was a dual cross ram four-barrel setup and air induction setup from a scooped hood.

tube headers on the engine for low restriction and high-power output. Chevrolet asked one of its big suppliers for a price on

Fig. 1-4. A special hood could be made functional; it took fresh air off the base of the windshield.

steel-tubing headers. The supplier, accustomed to working on 100,000-unit orders, came up with an initial estimate of $400, a price obviously not acceptable to Chevrolet, since you could buy headers for the 283/327 engine in any speed shop in the country for under $150. After finding a supplier that would make the headers at a more reasonable price, all 1967 Z28s did have steeltube headers. However, the headers were put in each car trunk for dealer or owner installation and all production line exhaust systems were standard cast-iron exhaust manifolds dumping out through dual exhausts.

Chevrolet rated the combination a ridiculously low 290 horsepower at 5800 rpm and 290 lb./ft. of torque at 4200 rpm. Early dyno tests of this combination showed it to be actually putting out close to 350 horsepower.

Other Z28 Features

Chevrolet didn't just throw a hot engine into the standard Camaro chassis, either. Components were matched throughout to give the Z28 buyer top road performance—almost the equivalent of Corvette performance at a much lower cost. Included in the Z28 package were, in addition to the special 302 engine which was not available in any other Chevrolet model, dual exhausts, special heavy-duty front and rear suspension components including shot-peened front ball studs, a rear radius rod to control rear-axle movement under hard acceleration, the previously mentioned viscous temperature-controlled fan, heavy-duty radiator, quick ratio steering, special 15 × 6 rally wheels with trim rings, 7.35 × 15 nylon, high-speed tires, a 3.73 rear axle ratio, and a pair of broad racing stripes on the hood and rear deck.

Additionally, there were several other options which were mandatory such as power front-disc brakes and a 4-speed close-ratio Muncie transmission with 2.20 low gear.

Total price of the Z28 option was $437.10 added to the Camaro's 1967 base price of $2572, so a Z28 could roll out the door in that first year for just $3314.60. Practically a miracle based on today's economy.

If you bought a Z28 Camaro, Chevrolet put certain restrictions on you as to other options you could also order on the car. For instance, no air conditioning was available, nor could you alter any suspension or chassis components. As we said, it was mandatory that you also order the 4-speed, close-ratio transmission and power front-disc brakes. There was another brake option which you could substitute if you didn't want the front discs—a special *heavy-duty* front disc brake package with metallic rear drum brakes. And it was highly recommended that you order the positraction limited-slip differential.

Bodywise, except for the racing stripes on the front hood and trunk lid, there was nothing special about the Z28, except for one little piece—a rear spoiler bolted onto the trunk lid. No one ever really knew whether the spoiler created any down force and really worked at higher speeds. But it looked racy as hell and that was part of the game.

Most of the first run of Z28s were built with the Rally Sports package. The RS option included items such as a full-width grill with concealed headlights, parking lights relocated in the valance, special moldings, some blacked-out trim and other accents to make the car even sportier looking. On cars that had both the Rally Sport and Z28 options, the Z28 emblems superseded the RS emblems that normally were installed on Rally Sport-equipped cars. In addition, many cars were built with a vinyl roof.

There were a couple of other noteworthy options that were available for Z28 buyers in 1967. The 3.73 axle ratio was standard. However, according to what the buyer was going to use the car for, he could choose from 3.07, 3.31, 3.55, 4.10, 4.56, and 4.88 rear-axle ratios. Manual steering with a 24-to-1 ratio was standard, but the buyer could choose manual steering with a faster 20-to-1 ratio, and power steering with 15.6-to-1 ratio was also available.

In October, 1967, a special production run of Regular Production Option Z28 1967 Camaros came off the assembly line, just in time to be approved for competition as of January, 1968. According to Chevrolet's own records, only 602 Z28 Camaros were manufactured on that special run. They never did build the 1000 needed to make the cars legal for the Trans Am series.

Of course, that didn't stop anybody from racing them, since Chevrolet had announced that they would make 1000 of them and everyone believed Chevrolet. All the people who raced in the Trans Am series in Z28s that year were doing so illegally, including Mark Donohue in the Sunoco Camaro owned by Roger Penske (Figs. 1-5 and 1-6). But nobody seemed to mind. Indeed, it was some of the best racing anyone had ever seen.

In *CAR and DRIVER's* road test of the '67 Z28, they recorded a standing start quarter mile of 14.9 seconds at 97 mph. Even more interesting, they recorded fuel mileage of 11 to 15 mpg. *CAR AND DRIVER's* testers called the 290 horsepower engine "without a

Fig. 1-5. Driver Mark Donohue accepts an award after driving the Z28 to the Trans-Am win.

doubt the most responsive American V8 we've ever tested." As you would expect, the review was favorable except for the

Fig. 1-6. Mark Donohue (left) drove and Roger Penske ran the team that dominated many race series including the Trans-Am in a Z28 during the late 1960s.

extremely loud exhausts, the flexing of the left-hand single-leaf spring (remember Chevrolet had only put one torque arm on the right side of the car), and some reservation about the brakes under severe conditions. Needless to say, any 1967 Z28 Camaro is now a collector's item.

THE 1968 REFINEMENTS

By the time the end of the 1967 model run was near and the '68 models had been introduced, Chevrolet had further refined the Z28 package and had given more choice to the Z-car buyer. For instance, for '68 you could order both a front and rear spoiler. And they actually worked. For the 1968 Z28 buyer, there were actually *four* Z28 Special Performance Packages as they were known. But Chevrolet still seemed in a quandary about the Z28.

At the same time they added performance options to the list available for Z28 buyers, they also dropped several items that would be of interest to the racer and relegated those to the status of dealer-installed. It seemed as though Chevrolet didn't know whether they wanted to market the car as a racing vehicle that was suitable for street driving or as a high-performance street machine which could be converted into a race car. The Z28 Camaro had been born a race car. And indeed, the Penske-prepared, Mark Donohue-driven '67 model had ripped the pants off the factory-backed Mustangs in the last two races of the 1967 Trans Am season, and had finished 1-2 in the Trans Am Class at Sebring in early 1968.

But in 1967, Chevrolet treated the Z28 as an illegitimate son. The car had been available for racing if you had the patience and perserverance to wait out the delivery of this rare animal. Yet, this fact had escaped many Chevrolet dealers. Some of Chevrolet's smaller dealers didn't even know such a package existed. Indeed, the Z28 was never mentioned in any 1967 sales brochure. The only mention of it was in a one-page sheet that was available at the 1967 Detroit auto show. The one-page sheet was entitled, "Camaro Coupe with Factory Option Z28" and this sheet was listed as a technical news bulletin from Chevrolet.

Obviously, Chevrolet felt that they had to have something to give to the public after displaying the car at the show. In fact, the sheet stated that the horsepower and torque rating of the 302 engine had not yet been determined nor had price been established for the Z28 option. So for many people, the Z28 was a cryptic symbol that wide-eyed enthusiasts murmured about to baffled sales personnel at many Chevrolet dealers.

The attitude continued into early 1968. For example, the 1968 Camaro sales brochure did not mention any such thing as a Z28 option, instead devoting pages to SS-396 Models, Rally Sports, and other "huggers from Chevrolet."

Chevrolet's marketing quandary was reflected in their ever-changing 1968 option list. At the beginning of the model year, they reflected the racing interest, but that philosophy changed as the model year wore on and the Z28 was made more accessible to more people.

As we mentioned, there were actually four Z28 Special Performance Packages offered in 1968. Special Performance Package Z28 consisted of the basic package plus a factory-installed, plenum air intake system, in other words, a cold air induction system. The list price of the standard Z28 package at the beginning of the 1968 model run was $400.25. A Z/282 with the fresh air intake system would set you back $479.25.

Then you could order Special Performance Package Z/283. This consisted of the standard Z28 package with a set of exhaust headers in the trunk. The price for the Z/283 package was $779.40. Obviously, Chevrolet didn't want to sell many of these packages, but if you wanted one, you could have it. The final Z28 setup was the Z/284, which was the standard Z28 package plus the installed fresh air intake system and the exhaust headers in the trunk. List price for Special Performance Package was $858.40. Again, a high price was applied apparently to discourage too many of these from getting into the wrong hands.

Buyers of '68 Z28s could also choose rear axle ratios up to 4.88-to-1 if they didn't like the standard 3.73. For the first time, there was also a transmission choice; either the wide-ratio, 4-speed (M20), close-ratio, 4-speed (M21) or the rock crusher, heavy-duty, close-ratio 4-speed (M22).

By the end of the 1968 model run, it was obvious that Chevrolet was serious about the Z28's performance, both on and off the race track, and in the showrooms, too. When the SCCA changed the rules for the Trans Am racing series to allow two 4-barrel carburetors and different cam shafts in place of the stock factory production items, Chevrolet quickly tooled up a cross ram, dual quad intake system that mounted twin 660 cfm Holley 4-barrels (Figs. 1-7 and 1-8) and a new camshaft that provided much more low-end torque.

Much research and development work was carried on for Penske and Donohue, not only at the General Motor's technical

Fig. 1-7. When used with the optional ram quad setup, the special air cleaner sealed against the hood.

center, but also at various race tracks around the country. Since Chevrolet was in the series anyway, management wanted the Penske-Donohue car to win and assigned certain engineers to help Donohue with various chassis and engine setups. Donohue drove

Fig. 1-8. Twin 800 cfm 4-barrels were used on the dual 4-barrel setup.

the blue Sunoco-Penske Camaro to a couple of tail end victories in the '67 series. In 1968, with the Chevrolet engineering talent at their disposal, the Penske-Donohue Camaro won 10 out of 13 races and the Trans Am series for Chevrolet (Fig. 1-9).

Meanwhile, on the street, the Z28 had already begun to make its mark (Figs. 1-10 and 1-11). The Chevrolet formula for success had never been as well executed: take a small, high-winding, high-output engine, mate it to a slick shifting 4-speed transmission, throw in a dose of high-performance chassis components and top it off with a stiff rear axle gear. Then go out and blow the doors off anything that comes near you. It had worked before in the early series Corvettes and it was working again for the Z28 Camaro. Guys were buying and building Z28s like mad. What also made it nice and interesting is the fact that many Corvette engine goodies fit the Z28. And that included all the special, small-block speed equipment that had been developed since 1955.

Also toward the end of the 1968 model run, Chevrolet had decided that it would make the Z28 much more accessible to a lot more potential buyers. A special Z28 brochure was whipped up and distributed to Chevrolet dealers.

Several important changes were made to the car itself to make it more acceptable in everyday transportation use. For instance, the single-leaf rear springs were gone, replaced by real automobile springs with multi leaves. Along with the new multi-leaf rear springs was a staggered shock arrangement that mounted the left shock behind the axle and the right shock in front of the axle. The staggering of the shocks controlled unwanted movement of the live rear axle and countered forces that twisted and wrapped up the leaf springs. The result was hard acceleration with little or no wheel hop.

Also standard on '68 Camaros were E70-15 wide-tread, low-profile tires in place of the original 7.35 × 15 red lines of 1967. And when the car was ordered with power steering and the mandatory power disc brakes, the resultant production package was very acceptable for everyday transportation, if the owner was willing to accept a certain amount of low-speed fussiness and lack of torque for easy take-off. Above 30 mph on winding mountain roadways, back country lanes and all the other types of roads which make driving worth doing, Z28 Camaro was an exhilirating vehicle. Handling with the fatter tires was excellent, cornering power was exceptional, and acceleration through the close ratio gears was amazing for a car powered by such a small engine.

Fig. 1-9. A Z28 won several SCCA Trans-Am championships during 1967-69 period.

There is something very satisfying about a small displacement engine producing big displacement power. You feel like the engine is doing something, not lumbering along wasting space and

Fig. 1-10. The interior of the '67-'69 models were luxurious for a car that could virtually be raced off the showroom floor. Note the poor placement of optional gauges low and forward on the console.

Fig. 1-11. The 1969 Z28 is considered one of the best of the series.

operating inefficiently. The Z28 engine was a jewel, an outstanding performer by any yardstick. And the chassis was even well-matched to the power plant. Suspension, drive train and brakes were all intended to complement the engine and all did an admirable job. No wonder the 7199 '68 Z28s are very much collectible today. In fact, purists consider the 1968 Z28 as the most desirable of all Z-cars, since it was the most refined of the earlier cars, had the most responsive engine and was still in the more trim 1967-68 body style.

THE 1969 Z28

In 1969 everyone discovered the Z28. Every major publication in the automotive field road tested at least one Z28 in 1969. Even Chevrolet brought the car completely out of wraps and showed a Z28 in its Camaro sales brochure. And the car came out of wraps with a new skin. Though bearing a strong family resemblance to the '67-68 Camaro, the '69 was a decidedly different car with a bolder, wider look that made it look both larger, and more purposeful (Fig. 1-12). Chevrolet was still calling the Camaro the Hugger, but the longer, wider, tougher, even quieter 1969 model was being billed as "the closest thing yet to a Corvette." And although the Camaro was finally coming into its own and being recognized as a road car to be reckoned with, Chevrolet was clearly moving it away from

21

racing and marketing it as an over-the-road performance GT machine.

For 1969, Chevrolet somewhat limited the new car Z28 buyer as far as options were concerned. The more exotic Z/282, Z/283, and Z/284 options were dropped from the option list. The individual pieces, however, were still available at your neighborhood Chevrolet dealer's parts counter. You could buy the parts and install them yourself, or have your dealer install them for you.

Meanwhile, only the basic Z28 Special Performance Package was available off the assembly line. The package remained as before: 302/290 high-performance V8, dual exhausts with low restriction mufflers, special heavy-duty front and rear suspension components, heavy-duty radiator and temperature-controlled fan, quick ratio steering, 15 × 7 rally wheels, E70 × 15 special, white-lettered tires, 3.73 ratio axle and special rally stripes for the hood and rear deck. As before, the Z28 package was available only with the mandatory 4-speed transmission and power disc brakes. And positraction was recommended. The Z28 Performance Package price for 1969 was $458.15.

Two important chassis changes are notable. Since the body had been restyled for 1969, the stylists had thoughtfully included larger wheel wells. This allowed wider wheels to be stuffed under the wheel wells and buyers benefited from the increased road adhesion. In place of the 15 × 7 wheels were the standard E70-15 fiberglass belted white-lettered tires. A new variable ratio power steering system was also introduced for 1969. The manual quick steering ratio was 21.4 to 1; however, the buyer could order the special N41 power steering option, which included super quick power steering with a ratio of 14.3-to-10.9.

Fig. 1-12. The 1969 Z28 featured a restyled body, fatter tires.

The 302's engine output remained the same—290 horsepower at 5800 rpm and 290 lb./ft. of torque at 4200 rpm. Just to give you an idea of how ridiculous that horsepower rating was, Chevrolet rated their mild 350 cubic inch hydraulic lifter motor at 300 horsepower that same year. The hydraulic lifter 350 engine had small ports, small valves, small 4-barrel carburetor on a low-rise cast iron intake manifold and a mild hydraulic lifter cam. Most knowledgeable enthusiasts were still saying that the stock Z28 302/290 engine was capable of at least 350 horsepower in stock trim.

As we mentioned, there was plenty of press on the 1969 Z28 Camaro. *CAR LIFE* road tested a Z28 with the optional dual 4-barrel intake setup and headers that were dealer-installed equipment. They recorded a 0 to 60 time of 7.4 seconds with the quarter mile coming up in 15.12 at 94.8 mph. This with a 4.10 rear axle ratio. The test results, slower than those obtained by their single 4-barrel 1968 test car, were explained away by the fact that dual 4-barrel intake setup was not meant for street use and actually decreased performance at low rpm.

CARS magazine road tested a similarly setup '69 Z28, except for a 4.56 rear axle gear and several nonstock suspension items which increased traction. Their results were spectacular: 0 to 60 in 5.5 seconds; quarter mile in 13.30 seconds at 106 mph. However, a quote from their road test is significant and telling: "the optional dual ram quad setup is a big waste for street use."

HOT ROD magazine also tested a Z28 in 1969. Their's was a more standard single 4-barrel stock model with a 4.56 rear axle ratio. Their results? Quarter mile in 14.34 seconds at 101.35 mph.

Clearly, the '69 Z28 could hold its own by any performance criteria. And, although sales were the best ever recorded, the Z28 was still being overshadowed by several other performance cars of that day. The year 1969 was the height of the muscle car era. The rule of the day was eyeball-sucking acceleration, spine-compressing 0 to 60 times, and simply sheer, brute horsepower. Even the Z28's 350 honest horsepower paled by comparison to some of the monster motors of 1969. If the car didn't have enough acceleration to peel back your eyelids, it just didn't cut the mustard back then. Of course, we'd do anything nowadays to have that kind of performance at a base price of $3443.80.

THE 1970 Z28 SECOND STAGE CAMARO

This was a confusing year for Chevrolet. Chevrolet had planned to introduce the completely restyled and re-engineered

Camaro at the beginning of the 1970 model year, that is, in October of 1969. This was impossible because of various production holdups. So the 1969 model was sold with no changes through February of 1970. When the 1969 model run finally ended, 20,302 1969 Z28 Camaros had been built. This was to be a sales record that held up for 10 years.

On February 26, 1970, John Z. DeLorean, Chevrolet Division General Manager, announced a totally new "second stage" Camaro. It was a totally new car (Fig. 1-13) from the ground up and looked it, with a silhouette that had a decidedly international flavor—longer hood, flatter windshield slope, swept-back roof line and a smooth, Corvette-type rear with twin tail lights. It was a knockout and could easily have passed for a Maserati or some other exotic European car. But it hadn't been built in Europe. It had been built in Detroit, and the new Camaro's Chevrolet heritage was quite evident beneath the skin.

The new Camaro extended the car's original concept closer toward the sports side of "sports-compact." It was now much less of a compact even though it still shared pieces with the Nova. Camaros were all fast-back coupes now, and interior room (Fig. 1-14) was better in both front and rear than it was in the former notchback coupe. Wheelbase was still 108 inches, but the overall length was two inches longer, and the car was 0.4-inch wider and 1.1 inches lower than the previous Camaro. The passenger compartment was over three inches farther back in the wheelbase than was the passenger compartment in the 1967-69 cars.

The windshield slope was greater and the total glass area was increased by nearly 10%. In addition, the glass ran high into the roofline, helping to increase forward visibility.

The drive-line tunnel was higher than before, and the center of the rear seat was eliminated as a result. The higher tunnel made possible a smoother ride by allowing for more rear suspension travel. The tunnel was almost a rear seat and center armrest. Front seat adjustment travel was now good enough to make driving comfortable for even those drivers over six feet tall—something the 1967-69 cars could never brag about.

Instruments were clustered in a wraparound panel directly in front of the driver. And on Z28s, when you ordered the special instrumentation package, all the gauges were on the instrument panel directly in front of the driver (Fig. 1-15), not down on the console as in previous years. Even the tach was built right into the instrument panel.

Chassis reworking consisted of larger side box rails on the separate front forward frame, and one large cross member replaced two small ones in the earlier design. Steering had been moved forward of the new cross member, too. To compensate for the inherent understeer characteristics of such an arrangement, a rear stabilizer bar was used on the optional suspensions and was standard on the Z28.

Multiple-leaf rear springs were continued, as were the staggered shocks. Front suspension was still the short and long A-arm independent design, but treated width was wider by 1.68 inches. Upper and lower control arm span had been increased a distance of 1.4 inches, a measure designed to reduce force concentration at the frame mounting points. Spindle length was also 1.4 inches longer, increasing the distance between ball joints. This reduced suspension component loadings. The front stabilizer bar diameter was 0.9375-inch, and Z28 cars also had a 0.688-inch diameter rear bar.

Fig. 1-13. In Feb. 1970, an entirely new Z28 was introduced with updated styling that many experts said rivaled the fine styling work of Ferrari and Maserati. It was definitely European looking. The chassis was updated, too.

For the first time, front disc brakes were standard, with power assist optional. Four-wheel disc brakes, offered optionally for a short period during the 1969 model run, were no longer offered as an option, nor were any of the other exotic racing options such as the fresh-air hood or special intake systems. Clearly, Chevrolet marketing was taking the road car approach rather than the race car approach.

The larger drive-shaft tunnel allowed an extra 0.75-inch of upward rear wheel travel. In addition, the jounce bumper, which is attached to the frame so that it snubs the axle when it's deflected all the way upward, was redesigned to give a progressive deflection-resistance rate—soft when the axle first contacts it and stiffer as it is compressed further. Thus, the driver didn't have to slow down so much now, perhaps not at all, when traversing dips and big bumps, to avoid having the rear axle bottom out. And when it did bottom, it wouldn't be with such a crash as before.

The increased wheel travel allowed the use of softer spring rates, particularly at the rear where excessively stiff springs were used previously both to discourage bottoming and to get adequate roll resistance. As we just mentioned, anti-roll stabilizer bars were used in the '70 to control roll stiffness rather than stiff springs.

Fig. 1-14. The 1970 interior featured European-styled buckets and a Porsche-like 4-spoke steering wheel.

Fig. 1-15. For the first time, all gauges in the '70 Z28 were right up on the dash where the driver could make good use of them.

There were changes in wheels and tires on the 1970 Camaros, too. The 15 × 7 wheel (Fig. 1-16) remained standard on the Z28. But extremely low profile F60-15 fiberglass belted tires were introduced as standard on the 1970 version. These flat tires really put the rubber down and increased handling and braking performance dramatically.

Again for '70, the Z28 Performance Package was available in both standard looking Camaro coupes and those equipped with the Rally Sport option. The standard Camaros came with a full-width front bumper that bisected the grill. But with the Rally Sport equipment group came a thoroughly European-looking front end with split front bumpers, Endura polyurethane grill shell, and parking turn signal lights that looked remarkably like driving lights. A Rally Sport equipped Z28 had to be one of the best looking cars to ever come out of Detroit.

But there was a lot more news in 1970 than simply a new body and some chassis changes. Under the hood lurked 48 additional cubic inches and 70 additional rated horsepower. The new standard engine for the Z28 was the LT-1 version of the 350 small block that was also offered in 1970 in the Corvette.

Although most of the pieces were interchangeable with earlier Chevrolet small block engines, most were designed for the new

27

1970 LT-1. The engine contained all your normal Chevrolet high-performance stuff including 4-bolt mains, forged aluminum pistons, big 800 cfm Holley carburetor, etc. But some pieces were all new. For instance, the cam shaft was a totally new grind that cut down the duration of the old 30-across cam and gave lots more low-end punch on the street with a slight sacrifice in all-out top-end horsepower. It was still a performance unit though, make no mistakes about that. And the solid lifters reminded you of that fact every three or four weeks when they asked you to adjust them.

The LT-1's heads were based on the old fuel injection heads and used the same valve sizes. However, ports were recontoured slightly for better flow and the old press-in studs were finally discarded for more modern screw-in studs. The 1970 Z28 engine was rated at 360 horsepower at 6000 rpm and 380 lb./ft. of torque at 4000 rpm.

Curiously, the identical engine in the Corvette was rated at 370 horsepower instead of 360. Zora Arkus Duntov just wouldn't let the Camaro have as much horsepower as his Corvette, even though they both used the same engine.

There's no doubt that these 90 extra lb./ft. of torque were felt on the street. When combined with the stock 3.73 rear axle ratio or any of the optional axle ratios, which ranged up to 4.10 for

Fig. 1-16. The 1970 wheels were seven inches wide with fat 60-series rubber for the first time.

assembly line installation, the Z28 could hold its own even against 400 cubic inch monster muscle cars.

Further reflecting Chevrolet's desire to have the Z28 appeal to a wider possible audience, for the first time you could order an automatic transmission in a Z28. Of course, it was the 3-speed turbo hydra-matic, and Z28s got the M40 heavy-duty version which really could bang off slick, quick shifts when asked to.

All that extra engine cost you more in 1970. The Z28 Special Performance Package was $572.95, up from $458.15 in '69. Even at close to $600, however, the Z28 engine was still one hell of a bargain. As before, the package wasn't just an engine. It was a *whole* package, from the trim right down to the chassis.

Chevrolet's 1970 Camaro brochure highlighted the Z28 as never before with four full pages of photos and information on the car. The sales catalog admonished potential buyers as follows:

"When you come to see the Z, make sure you've got your driving gloves." It then went on to say that if the equipment offered as part of the Z28 wasn't enough "to get your adrelanine flowing, there's a Corvette catalog not too far away." And with Corvettes priced at $2500 more at least, Chevrolet figured they would get plenty of buyers who really wanted a Corvette but would be willing to settle for just the performance level of a Corvette in a Camaro body. And that's what the 1970 Z28 offered.

The praise for the new Z28 was almost universal (Fig. 1-17). Even though *CAR AND DRIVER* recorded a 0 to 60 time of 5.8 seconds for the car and covered the quarter mile in 14.2 seconds at 100.3 mph, they said that, "Somehow, though, the Z28 is not as thrilling as it once was. It's more tolerant to driving techniques now, more mature in its behavior. All things considered, it's a better engine now, but the loss of a carefree and irresponsible adolescent spirit can never be witnessed without some regret." *CAR LIFE's* test car was a hair slower than *CAR AND DRIVER's*, recording a 6.5 0 to 60 time and the quarter mile in 14.51 seconds at 98.79 mph. They noted that the car was a lot more civilized to drive now, too, and said that "the Z28 is as close to a mild mannered racing car as the industry has come." *HOT ROD* magazine, testing a 4-speed version, recorded a quarter mile of 14.93 seconds at 97 mph. And the *HOT ROD* tester complained that the suspension was too soft!

Happily for Chevrolet, 8733 people disagreed and bought the car. This was more than had purchased the 1968 version but far short of the record set the year before.

THE 1971 Z28

Nineteen seventy-one was the year of the General Motors' edict on lower compression ratios and not even performance cars like the Z28 escaped the required change. Although the rest of the package remained the same (remember, it had been introduced only six months before), lowering the compression ratio from 11.0 to 9.0 to 1 obviously had its effect on the Z's performance capabilities. The horsepower of the lower compression LT-1 was now pegged at 330 at 5600 rpm with the torque called 360 lb./ft. at 4000 rpm.

The rest of the Z28 Special Performance Package was identical to that introduced just a few months before as the new 1970 model. In fact, the car was so identical that Chevrolet didn't even bother to change the copy in their dealer showroom brochure, merely substituting a different photo for the one in the 1970 brochure.

Fig. 1-17. The author after a test session with two of the new 1970 Z28s.

Even though the car was the same (Figs. 1-18 and 1-19), except for the lowered horsepower of the LT-1 engine, that didn't stop Chevrolet from raising the price of the Z28 option to $786.75. The higher price tag on the option may have had something to do with sales, which dropped nearly in half to 4863 Z28 units in 1971.

THE 1972 Z28

By the 1972 model year, both the price tag and the curb weight of the Camaro were climbing at an alarming rate. Even though the car itself hadn't changed substantially since 1970 in mechanical specification, remember that more and more safety and pollution devices were being Federally-mandated each year. So the car was gaining weight in that regard. In addition, the Camaro was continually upgraded in trim, making it a more luxurious, comfortable GT road car (Fig. 1-20).

Although neither the engine nor the car changed one iota for 1972, except for the inclusion of Federally-mandated safety and emission equipment, the Z28 suffered almost irreparable damage to its image. This was the first year of Federally-mandated SAE net horsepower ratings. Although the engine was still the robust solid lifter performer it was the year before (Fig. 1-21), the net horsepower rating brought the published figure down from 330 to 255 horsepower at 5600 rpm, while the torque went from 360 to 280 lb./ft. at 4000 rpm. Not only did the Z-car's image suffer, but so did the buyer's wallet. The price of the Z28 Special Performance Package rose to $769.05 by 1972, with no end of price rises in sight.

The only mechanical change of significance was the offering of three manual transmissions, in addition to the 3-speed turbo hydra-matic. The standard close ratio 4-speed with 2.20 low gear and M22 rock crusher heavy-duty 4-speed were joined by a 2.52 low gear wide ratio 4-speed for those who wanted more street flexibility in their Z28's driving characteristics. Both 3.73 and 4.10 axle ratios were continued.

Again, Z28 sales were cut almost in half from the year before, down to 2575 units. This was the lowest total yet since 1968.

THE 1973 Z28

This was a year of change for the Z28 (Fig. 1-22). The car and chassis remained essentially the same. But under the hood, the engine change was drastic. Gone was the LT-1 high-performance solid lifter engine, the victim of emission controls that had all but strangled the life out of the engine. In its place was the L82,

Fig. 1-18. The 1971 Z28 was virtually unchanged, and with a solid lifter 350 engine it could make tracks.

somewhat of an emasculation of the LT-1 but still a hot performer compared to other smog motors. The 4-bolt main block remained, as did the high-flow cylinder heads. But the hot solid lifter cam was replaced by a much milder hydraulic unit. The high-rise aluminum intake manifold went the way of all flesh, as did the big Holley 4-barrel carb. Standard setup on the L82 was a low rise cast iron intake manifold and Rochester Quadrajet 4-barrel carb. All this in the name of better emission control.

Fig. 1-19. Since the 1970 was on sale for only about six months, Chevrolet kept the styling the same for 1971. Why mess up a good thing? A Z28 trademark: the wide stripes on the hood and deck, were retained.

Fig. 1-20. What many consider to be the most beautiful Z28 ever. The 1972 model with Rally Sport option, which gave the buyers the small bumpers and clean grille. A neat car. And very collectible.

The controls themselves didn't do much good for the performance output of the L82 engine. But there was nothing anyone could do to get out of that one. The 1973 L82 powered Z28 Camaro was rated 245 horsepower at 5200 rpm and 280 lb./ft. of torque at 4000 rpm. Gone was the spine-compressing acceleration of the '68 and '69 solid lifter Zs. But things weren't that bad. In place of the spine-compressing acceleration, you had street tractability, more luxury and comfort than ever before, and you could even order air conditioning in your Z-car for 1973!

When air was ordered, the rear axle ratio was dropped from 3.73 to 3.42 regardless of transmission. And positraction was now standard equipment.

Fig. 1-21. A '72 Z28 during a test session for *Cars Magazine* at Raceway Park in Englishtown, NJ. The car performed superbly.

The Federal government also influenced the way the 1973 Z28 looked. If you ordered your car before the January 1, 1973 deadline, you could still opt for the chromeless, bumperless Rally Sport front-end package. All cars built after January 1, 1973, had to have the Federally-mandated 5 mph bumper that was standard equipment on all Camaros (Fig. 1-23). Compared to the sleek looking, lean Rally Sport front end, the standard 1973 front end looked heavy and crude by comparison. In retrospect, though, it doesn't look bad at all. In fact, it looks pretty damn good.

Because the L82 engine was a lot cheaper to produce than the old solid lifter LT-1, the price tag for the Z28 Special Performance Package dropped several hundred dollars in 1973. If you ordered a Z28 in a plain old Camaro sport coupe, the price tag was $598 extra. If you were opting for a luxury Type LT coupe, the Z28 package would cost you only $502 extra.

Perhaps it was the lower price tag. Perhaps it was the realization by car enthusiasts everywhere that their buying choices were becoming severely limited in the marketplace. The day of the car was already over. So if you wanted a really high-performance car, there weren't too many choices left, the Camaro Z28 being one of them. Whatever it was, sales surged in 1973 to 11,575 units—the highest total since 1969.

Road test results for the 1973 Z28 were generally good, although a far cry from the brute horsepower days of the late '60s. *CAR CRAFT* road tested a 4-speed version that covered the quarter mile in 14.69 seconds at 96 mph.

We personally had the opportunity to road test a '73 Z28 Camaro that had been tuned by Briggs Chevrolet in South Amboy,

Fig. 1-22. The '74 was one of the best handling cars the author had ever tested. Here he pushes the car through a tight turn at the Bridgehampton Race Circuit.

Fig. 1-23. The 1973-74 Z28s were almost identical. 1973 was the first year of Federal 5 mph bumpers, so the Rally Sport no-bumper look was gone forever.

New Jersey. In those days, Briggs Chevrolet was certainly the premier Chevrolet high-performance dealership in the nation, and they had dynotuned our test car to perfection. In addition to a full load of luxury items including air conditioning, our L82 power test car also had had a 4.10 rear axle gear set installed in place of the 3.42 stock gearing. In addition, the 3-speed turbo hydra-matic had been sharpened up with a bang shift plate which hardened up the shift points and made them almost instantaneous. Zero to 60 came up in a quick 5.6 seconds and the quarter mile in 14.19 seconds at 96 mph.

THE 1974 Z28

There were few changes for 1974. A 3.73 axle ratio was made standard regardless of the transmission, but a 3.42 ratio was installed when air conditioning was ordered. There were no optional axle ratios. In addition, power steering became standard on the Z28. Power brakes had been made standard the year before, as had a positraction limited-slip differential. Also new was a 21 gallon fuel tank to increase the driving range of the Z28. Bold new striping for the hood and deck lid (Figs. 1-24, 1-25, 1-26) completed the package. For 1974, the Z28 Special Performance Package remained priced at $502 extra on the LT and $573 extra on a standard sport coupe model.

In the April, 1974, issue of *CARS*, the magazine awarded the Z28 its Performance Car of the Year award. Frankly admitting that its job was easier than in past years because of the dearth of real performance cars, the magazine's editors nevertheless lauded the Z28 for its superior over-the-road performance and handling.

This writer took part in the selection of the Z28 as the award winner that year, and we wrote the road test that appeared in the award issue. The Z28 was as quick and fast a car as you were able to buy in 1974, and our test car ran the quarter mile in 14.8 seconds at 93 mph with a 4-speed transmission (Fig. 1-27). But where the Z28 really stoodout was not only on the drag strip but on the ride and handling course.

Fig. 1-24. New hood graphics were an option in 1974 with a large Z28 callout.

Fig. 1-25. The 1974 Z28 graphics were carried through to the rear deck when ordered. This particular car had the high trim Type LT interior option.

There's no question that by 1974, Chevrolet's engineers had sorted out the Camaro's chassis to the point where the Z28 suspension combination really got the job done—in spades! The quick ratio power steering allowed you to put the car any place you wanted and the suspension was so good that transient response was most unreal. Steering was almost neutral with just a hint of understeer changing gradually to a slight hint of oversteer at the limit.

In the Z-car it was easy to look like a professional driver. Even difficult corners became easy meat for the excellent Z suspension

Fig. 1-26. The 1974 Z28 package could be had with or without the loud hood graphics. Here are three '74s pictured at Westhampton Dragstrip after a test session which resulted in the car being chosen Performance Car Of The Year by *Cars Magazine*.

Fig. 1-27. Zero to 60 time average under seven seconds in 1974 with L-82 350 engine, automatic and 3.73 gears.

system. The car was easily controlled in any attitude and you had to be a real lummox to lose it. However, you *could* lose it. The L82 engine generated enough torque so that injudicious use of the throttle at the wrong time in a corner would quickly bring on power oversteer. And if you stayed on it, you would quickly be looking at where you just came from. Even up to the point of losing it, however, simply lifting your right foot would tuck the tail back in and you could simply motor on through. The flat wide-bias belted tires generated super cornering power and slid gradually in an easily controlled fashion. It was simple to play road racer in a Z-car.

The suspension was firm as in any good road car (Fig. 1-28). But Chevrolet's suspension engineers had learned the European secret of firm suspension with suspension travel. This allowed the Z28 Camaro to not only give strong cornering power under any conditions but also absorb road imperfections without jarring the kidneys of its occupants. We thought the Z28 suspension was as good as any live axle car we had ever driven, and we'd driven lots of cars up to that time (Fig. 1-29 and 1-30).

Admittedly, the Z28 package had been designed originally for the race track. However, by 1974 it had evolved into not a race car package but more a GT road machine package in the tradition of the world's great GT cars such as the Ferrari Daytona and Maserati Ghibli. We're not saying the 1974 Z28 Camaro was a Ferrari or a Maserati. But on the road, it gave you the same general feel and similar driving satisfaction as either of those great cars. Appa-

Fig. 1-28. A good suspension setup allowed the Z28 to come storming off the line with good traction.

rently, lots of people agreed with us because Chevrolet sold 13,802 1974 Z28s.

Fig. 1-29. The rear deck spoiler has always been both attractive and functional on the Z28.

But then, with the pressures of the Arab oil embargo, emission control freaks, Washington bureaucratic zealots and the safety fanatics breathing down their necks, Chevrolet's management panicked and dropped the ball. There was no Z28 Camaro in 1975, 1976, and half way through the 1977 model run. Chevrolet had dropped the ball and severely misread the market for performance cars.

Fig. 1-30. Downforce helps the Z28 maintain traction at high speeds.

So from '75 through mid '77, Chevrolet had nothing but a tape and paint cosmetic package called the Rally Sport to satisfy the performance enthusiast car buyer who was still out there but had nothing to buy in Chevrolet dealer's showrooms across the nation.

By contrast, Pontiac's management had also considered the idea of dropping their premier performance car, the Trans Am Firebird, but decided against it. Their reward was steadily building sales of the Trans Am model and a permanent hold on first place in the sporty car performance image marketplace.

THE 1977 Z28

Almost as soon as the car was dropped, Chevrolet enthusiasts began screaming for its return. Chevrolet's management hesitated, trying to read the gas-starved performance car market correctly. Finally, during the 1977 model year, and with Pontiac's Trans Am sales rapidly rushing toward the magical 100,000 units per year level, Chevrolet re-introduced the Z28.

At a press conference in Daytona Beach just before the 500 mile NASCAR race, and the International Race of Champions (IROC) event, Robert D. Lund, Chevrolet General Manager, made the announcement that the Camaro Z28 was indeed back:

"We firmly believe the Z28 may well prove to be the best handling production vehicle ever built," said Lund, "and that it will set a new standard for production cars of the future. We haven't compared it to all the foreign cars in detail, but we have no reason to believe there is a better handling vehicle anywhere."

Lund stated that unprecedented demand for the Camaro and recent changes in the specialty vehicle market made the decision to reactivate the Z28 obvious to Chevrolet product planners several months before (Fig. 1-31).

"The Camaro Z28 is intended for the macho enthusiast," he said. "It is a driver's car. Today, the enthusiast wants a special breed of aspiration car. He wants a car with functional sophistication and with finesse. He wants his car to be aggressive, quick, agile and dependable. He is very critical and we welcome his appraisal of the Z28."

The new Z28 offered as standard equipment the Chevrolet LM-1 350 cubic inch 4-barrel engine and a 4-speed heavy-duty Borg Warner transmission with an 11-inch high-capacity clutch and 2.64 first gear ratio. A high shift point, 3-speed turbo hydramatic 350 transmission was optional. Rear axle ratio with the manual transmission was 3.73 to 1, and with the automatic, 3.42 to 1 (Fig. 1-32).

More efficient power output was achieved with an open exhaust system using dual resonators in place of mufflers. This reduced exhaust system back pressure by 40% at 4000 rpm. The exhaust system still used a single catalytic converter, however, which kept power down to 170 horsepower at 3800 rpm and 270 lb./ft. of torque at 2400 rpm. Compression ratio was 8.5 to 1.

Refined revalving of shock absorbers, rather than the traditional heavy-duty type shocks, helped maintain wheel control on hard, rough corners. This, combined with higher spring rates, helped to minimize driver bounce and fatigue usually associated with sporty cars, particularly on long freeway trips.

Suspension system components were designed using special GR70-15 steel-belted radial tires and 15 × 7 wheels. Development engineers changed the front and rear stabilizer bars, spring rates, rear spring shackles and shock valving to provide balanced, linear handling in all driving modes. The front suspension featured springs with a rate of 365 lb./in. rate and a 1.20-inch anti-roll stabilizer bar. The rear suspension had springs with a rate of 127 lb./in. and a .55-inch stabilizer bar.

More precise steering was also accomplished by reducing the overall steering ratio from the standard Camaro's 16 to 1 down to 14 to 1. Power assist on both steering and brakes was standard equipment.

The Z28 appearance package included front and rear spoilers, body colored bumpers, rally wheels, and color-keyed sport mirrors. Complementing the seven available exterior colors were specific Z28 accent decals for the hood, front fender, front and rear spoiler, wheel opening and rocker panel (Figs. 1-33 and 1-34). In

Fig. 1-31. The newly re-introduced Z28 in 1977. The car was first displayed to the press before the Daytona 500 stock car race in Florida, then at the Chicago Auto Show.

Fig. 1-32. At re-introduction in 1977, Chevrolet displayed all the parts on the new Z28 that differed from the stocker Camaro components.

addition, Z28 decal emblems adorned the grill, rear-end panel and front fenders. Black painted grill, rear-end panel, parking and headlamp bezels, and black front and rear reveal and wheel opening moldings were also used. According to Lund, initial Z28 production was at an annual rate of from 20,000 to 25,000 units, but could be adjusted considerably higher to suit the man. The suggested base price of this new Z28 was $5,170.60. As it turned out, Chevrolet was able to build only 1833 units before the 1977 model year ended.

THE 1978 AND 1979 Z28s

As could be expected, the press loved the newly introduced 1978 Z28 (Fig. 1-35) and kept asking the question, "What took you

Fig. 1-33. Styling from the rear of the 1977 Z28 is very similar to the last '74 versions. The rear backlite is larger, and the wheels are color keyed to the body.

so long, Chevrolet?" Unfortunately, the LM-1 engine was a mere shell of any of the performance engines that had gone before in Z28s. Although the higher numerical rear axle gearing helped the car's straight line performance, any acceleration comparisons between this newly introduced Z28 and previous Z28s were meaningless.

What did come in for much praise were the handling characteristics of the car. And while almost every road test said that the Z28 handling characteristics were fantastic, there was always the faint shadow of Pontiac's Trans Am hanging over the car. That 2½ year absence from the market place could not be ignored. Clearly, in the minds of the automotive press, the Trans Am would forever more be the benchmark for performance levels for sporty cars. Sadly, the Z28 was relegated to the role of trying to meet the performance levels of the Trans Am rather than setting them as it had always done in years past.

Fig. 1-34. The '77 featured a front spoiler, radial 70-series tires and an unfortunate decal hood scoop.

44

Fig. 1-35. The 1978 Z28. A clean design with an integral lower front bumper in place of the stick-on front spoiler of the previous year.

In 1978, potential buyers wandering into a Chevrolet dealership were greeted with a Z28 right smack on the cover of the 1978 Camaro sales brochure. No longer would the Z28 ever be buried on one or two pages on the back of the brochure. Now the Z28 was clearly the performance leader of the Chevrolet pack and Chevrolet was clearly going to make sure that everyone knew it.

Several refinements could be found on the 1979 Z28. All Camaros shared a new soft fascia front and rear bumper system (Fig. 1-36). The soft front end gave full front bumper impact protection without the appearance of a heavy, wide bumper. In place of the tacky hood scoop decal found on the '77½ Z28, a real molded fiberglass (nonfunctional) hood scoop was added to the '78 models (Fig. 1-37). In addition, functional front fender louvres were added in place of louvre decals. Optional 15 × 7 aluminum wheels were also added to the option list. The new standard tire was a high-pressure P-metric steel-belted radial, size P225/70R15, with raised white letters.

The power brake system was provided with added protection by a charcoal filter. The new filtering unit was located in the vacuum supply line running from the engine to the brake booster assembly. Thus, gaseous fumes, such as fuel vapors that might be detrimental to booster function, were absorbed by the charcoal.

The brake pressure differential switch, mounted in the brake fluid distributor assembly, was now made of nylon material in place of steel. The nylon housing prevented corrosion and provided a better fluid seal with the cast iron distributor housing.

Fig. 1-36. In 1978, Chevrolet restyled the front end of the Z28, taking styling cues from the Berlinetta show car with a soft fascia and the bumperless look.

New frame reinforcements which tied into the front suspension cross member increased front end rigidity, while new rear spring shackles limited rear axle transverse movement and produced a more positive response and firmer handling feel. The handling improvement was further increased for all models with an

Fig. 1-37. Side view clearly shows the functional fender louvers substituted for the decals of the 1977 car. Hood scoop, while not functional, was at least a bolt-on fiberglass piece instead of a decal.

Fig. 1-38. Rear view shows redesigned tail lights and new bumpers painted body color.

added center bolt attachment from the reinforcement to the lower control arm bracket.

Fig. 1-39. Another front end redesign marked the 1979 Z28. The new 3-piece air dam and front wheel opening flares gave the Z a racier appearance. Striping and wheels were new, too.

Lastly, a new optional see-through lift-out roof panel, similar to those on the Corvette, was added to the option list for all Camaros including Z28s.

Under the hood the LM-1 engine came in for a little bit of attention, too. Thanks to a new cold air duct on the intake side and more efficient exhaust ports, high rpm breathing was helped considerably. The engine for 1978 was rated 185 horsepower at 4000 rpm with 280 lb./ft. of torque at 2400 rpm.

In *CAR AND DRIVER's* road test of the car, they recorded a 7.3 second 0 to 60 time and covered the quarter mile in 16 seconds flat at 91.1 mph. Top speed was an actual 123 mph. Clearly the acceleration was off from previous years, but the car was up to the performance levels of its competition. Customers thought so, too, because the 1978 Camaro was purchased by 54,907 people. That's almost triple the previous high total for any Z28 model.

The only change for 1979 (Figs. 1-38 and 1-39) was a new 3-piece front air dam and front wheel opening flares for a bolder appearance that complemented the rear deck lid spoiler. The air dam was semi-flexible plastic and included special Z28 striping that blended with the side striping to the car. Chevrolet expected to sell 85,500 Z28s in 1979.

The 1980 Z28

For 1980, there were several significant changes to the Z28, both mechanically and cosmetically, that should be documented. Finally, after decals and bolt-on fiberglass replicas of scoops and ports had been used since the car's re-introduction in 1977, Chevrolet broke down and made all the scoops and ports on the car functional for the first time. Both the hood air intake and fender ports now really did duct cool air into their respective areas (Fig. 1-41). The hood air intake provided additional outside ambient air to the engine, which measurably benefited engine performance during acceleration. The rearward-facing air intake door was solenoid-actuated and triggered electrically by a switch connected to the accelerator pedal. At steady speeds, the air door remained closed. But when you nailed the throttle and punched it, the door flopped open to admit large gulps of cooler outside air to the engine (Fig. 1-42). Although Z28 enthusiasts everywhere were glad to see Chevrolet make the car more functional and less Mickey Mouse, the fact is that Pontiac's Trans-Am had had the same feature on their shaker hood scoop back in 1973. Also made functional were the fender ports which now provided a side exit path for heated

Fig. 1-40. The 1980 Z28.

engine compartment air. Other features are shown in Figs. 1-43, 1-44 and 1-45.

Also juggled slightly were the spring rates and steering ratio. The standard power steering now had a gear ratio of 14 to 1 and an overall ratio of 13 to 1 on the Z28, which was actually a little slower than the variable ratio setup on standard Camaros. Lock to lock required 2.61 turns on the Z and 2.41 on all other Camaros. Chevy engineering figured that with a car this responsive, a slightly slower steering response would keep the maniacs out of trouble. The spring rates had been altered slightly in the middle of the 1979 model run, with the computer making more precise matches of spring rates to individual cars and their option load. The base rates were 365 lb./in. for the front coils and 140 lb./in. for the rear leaves. These rates were carried over into 1980.

If you were a Z28 buyer in 1980 and you lived in California, you were in for a rude shock when you walked into your neighborhood

Fig. 1-41. The '80 Z28 features a look that will make it hard to distinguish a '79 from an '80, except by virtue of new paint colors.

Fig. 1-42. The air scoop on the 1980 Z-car was functional. When the throttle was punched, the rear flap flopped open to admit cold air to the carburetor.

Chevy dealer's showroom. Because of ever-stringent emission control regulations, especially in California where they'd had their own set of laws for years, the LMI 350 cubic inch engine was no longer available in the Z28 after the 1979 model year.

Fig. 1-43. Cast aluminum spoke wheels were an addition for 1980. P-metric steel belted radials were made standard in 1979.

Fig. 1-44. A new grille made the '80 a hairy looking street machine.

So if you wanted a Z-car in California, you had to take it with the LG4 305 cubic inch 4-barrel engine or forget it altogether. In fact, the only combination available for sale in California in 1980 was the 305 engine, automatic transmission and 3.42 axle ratio. You had no other choice. Buyers in the other 49 states had their choice of either the automatic or wide ratio 4-speed transmission. If you opted for the automatic, you got the turbo hydra-matic 350 and 3.42 rear axle ratio. Four-speed buyers got a 3.42 ratio first gear in the transmission, teamed with a 3.08 axle ratio.

The LMI engine sold in the other 49 states remained virtually unchanged as did the 305 engine from previous years in other Chevrolet products (Fig. 1-46). The engine had a compression ratio of 8.6 to 1 and breathed through a single Rochester 4-barrel carburetor. This special 4-barrel version of the 305 was not available anywhere else in the country and, in fact, was available only in California the year before also. The version of the 305 available in the other 49 states used a single 2-barrel carb (engine designated LG3).

In addition, the LG4 305 utilized the C4 emission control system; C4 stands for *computer controlled catalytic converter*. It is essentially a 3-way catalytic converter system that controls all three measured pollutants—HC, CO and NOx. By means of exhaust sensors and sensors in other parts of the fuel system, the computer controls precisely the air-fuel ratio of the engine, thereby resulting in more efficient combustion and cleaner air out the exhaust. Beginning in 1981, the C4 system was added to all General Motors cars as standard equipment.

Despite the ever lowered acceleration and top speed levels, and despite ever escalating costs, Chevrolet still expected to sell over 100,000 Z28 Camaros in 1980 (Fig. 1-47).

The Z28 is finally getting the attention from car enthusiasts that it has deserved since 1967. Most car enthusiasts have grown

Fig. 1-45. Rear view of the 1980 model. Note the blacked-out tail light section and optional hatch roof.

Fig. 1-46. Although Californians had to be content with a 305 4-barrel engine in 1980, the rest of the country could still count on 350 cubes under the hood and enough poke to spin the rear tires.

up lusting after, owning, or, in our case, testing Z28s year after year for over a decade. It is practically the charter member of America's performance hall of fame. The latest Z28s bring car enthusiasts everywhere the best rounded Z28 ever. The knife edge of acceleration and handling is blunted; but ride, styling and interior comfort are all honed to a new brilliance. The Z28: An inspiring, precision machine that allows you to enjoy something that has been so often missing on the automotive scene for a long time—the sheer enjoyment of driving.

Fig. 1-47. A 1980 Z28 running at the GM Proving Grounds in Milford, Michigan. Still a pretty sight for Z-car enthusiasts.

Chapter 2
Z-Power
Engine Spotter's Guide

Since its introduction in 1967, Chevrolet has used four basic engines to power the Z28. For those readers interested in greater detail than that found in Chapter 1, here's a short guide to the characteristics of each of those four engines.

THE 302/290 ENGINE

The 302 cubic inch engine (Fig. 2-1) was used in Z28s in the years 1967, '68, and '69. The engine is rated at 290 horsepower at 5800 rpm and 290 lb./ft. of torque at 4200 rpm.

Bore and stroke are 4.00 inches by 3.00 inches. Compression ratio is 11.0 to 1. The carburetor is a single 4-barrel Holley. The carburetors used in 1967 are one of four model numbers: 3943, 3944, 3910 or 3911. The 1968 and '69 carburetor is a Holley model number R-4053-A. Both the primary and secondary throttle bodies measured 1.686 inches.

Proper timing for the '67 engine is 2° BTDC at 900 rpm. For '68 and '69 engines, the proper timing is 4° BTDC at 900 rpm. The camshaft part number for this engine is 3849346.

Basically, this engine, except for the shortstroke 283 crankshaft, is simply the 327 fuel injection engine with a carburetor in place of the fuel injection system. Included as components in this engine with the high-strength 4-bolt main block are forged crank and pistons, high-flow heads with large 2.02-inch intake valves and 1.60-inch exhaust valves, solid lifter cam, high-rise aluminum intake manifold and the aforementioned Holley 4-barrel carburetor.

THE 350/360 LT-1 ENGINE

The LT-1 engine (Fig. 2-2) was used in Z28 Camaros in 1970 in both the older and new 70½ body styles, then again in 1971 and 1972. The 1970 engine is rated 360 horsepower at 6000 rpm with torque rated 380 lb./ft. at 4000 rpm. The 350 cubic inch engine has a 4.001-inch bore and 3.484-inch stroke. Compression ratio is 11 to 1 and the carburetor is a single 4-barrel Holley carburetor, model numbers 4484-1A or 45555-A on stick shift cars and 4454-1A or 4490-A on cars equipped with automatic transmissions. The primary and secondary throttle openings measured 1.6875 inches. Correct timing for these engines is 8° BTDC at 800 rpm on stick-shift models and at 650 rpm in drive for automatics.

The 1971 engine remained the same, except for different pistons which lowered the compression ratios from 11 to 1 to 9 to 1. The horsepower rating of the '71 engine is 330 at 5600 rpm and torque is rated 360 lb./ft. at 4000 rpm. The cam shaft remained the same—PN3972182—with solid lifters.

Although there was no change to the engine itself in 1972, the method of rating horsepower was changed from gross to SAE net. As such, the LT-1's horsepower rating is 255 horsepower at 5600 rpm and torque was rated 280 lb./ft. at 4000 rpm.

Fig. 2-1. The 302/290 engine used in 1967-68.

THE 350 L-82 ENGINE

The 1973 and '74 Z28s use an engine known as the L-82 (Fig. 2-3). It is primarily a desmogged LT-1 with the same 4-bolt main block and the high-flow cylinder heads with 2.0 intake valves; but the hot solid-lifter camshaft has been replaced by a milder hydraulic unit. Also changed was the intake setup. The L-82 uses a low-rise cast iron intake manifold and a standard Rochester Quadrajet 4-barrel carburetor as found on virtually every other Chevrolet 4-barrel engine. The 1973 and '74 Z28 Camaro engine is rated 245 horsepower at 5200 rpm and 280 lb./ft. of torque at 4000 rpm. The compression ratio is 8.2 to 1.

THE 350 LM-1 ENGINE

From 1977 through 1980 models, the Z28 uses the LM-1 350 cubic inch engine (Fig. 2-4). This is a relatively mild hydraulic lifter engine with an 8.2 to 1 compression ratio and one 4-barrel Rochester Quadrajet on a cast iron intake manifold. In 1977, the compression ratio was reduced to 8.5 to 1 and the rated horsepower is 170 at 3800 rpm. Torque is 270 lb./ft. at 2400 rpm.

For the years 1978 through '80, the compression ratio was dropped slightly to 8.2 to 1. But a less restricted intake system and cold air duct into the carburetor added horsepower to the rating which is 185 horsepower at 4000 rpm. Torque remained at 280 lb./ft. at 2400 rpm.

Fig. 2-2. The 350 LT-1 engine used in 1969-72.

Fig. 2-3. The 350 L-82 engine used in 1973-74.

Fig. 2-4. The 350 LM-1 engine used in 1977-80.

In contrast to previous years, the LM-1 engine is found in several other Chevrolet models, including Impalas, Caprices, other Camaros and Novas, and is the base engine in the Corvette.

THE 305 LG-4 ENGINE

In California beginning in 1980, the LG-4 was used as a substitute engine for Z28s because the standard LM-1 could not pass the stringent California emission control regulations.

The 305 has a bore/stroke of 3.736 in./3.48 in. It is an integral part of the Chevy small-block engine family, which means that many parts are interchangeable from other small block engines. Compression ratio is 8.6 to 1. The carburetor is a single Rochester Quadrajet 4-barrel which incorporates a closed-loop computer system to work in conjunction with the computer-controlled catalytic converter (C4) system. The carburetor part number is 17080502. The engine also uses an air injection pump to help control emissions.

Chapter 3

Supertuning For The Street

As good as the Z28 engines have been as far as performance is concerned, there's always room for improvement. That's because factory engineers have to compromise their tuning priorities for many different things: emissions, fuel economy and noise being among them. Maximum performance is often down on the list. And if you've driven a late model automobile, you know that driveability is often sacrificed for emission control.

Happily, as the owner of a Z28, you can make quite a substantial improvement in the car's overall response, efficiency, driveability and performance with a minimum of effort and a few simple tools. Although the changes involved are simple in nature, they can make quite a difference in actual performance. If you had the opportunity to actually measure the performance over a timed course, you'd find that these simple changes could knock up to a half second from your 0 to 60 time, and a half second off your quarter mile ET, while raising your quarter mile trap speed an average of 5 mph. In other words, they work. But before we get going, a few words of caution.

The changes outlined here are not for the earlier 302 cubic inch Z28 engine. First of all, all those cars are now collector's items that should be kept stock if they are to be appreciated in coming years. Secondly, those cars had special components which are not discussed here, such as dual-point distributors. Thirdly, few were built anyway.

The tuning procedures we discuss here are suitable for the later LT-1 350 engine, but they work even better on the 350 L-82 and latest 350 LM-1 engines. So if you have one of these 350 engines in your Z28, you'll really benefit from supertuning.

LEGAL RAMIFICATIONS

Before we get into supertuning, here's one other note of caution: The modifications in any supertune render some of the emission controls ineffective. In some states, it's illegal to remove or render ineffective any factory-installed emission control device. In other states, they don't care what you do to your car. If you intend to supertune your own Z28 engine, or any engine for that matter, check with local officials of your highway patrol before going ahead.

It is a Federal offense for any new car dealer or manufacturer to remove or render inoperative the emission controls on any car before it is sold to the customer. This means you can't ask a new car dealer to perform your supertune. It is not illegal to have an independent repair shop or tuner do this work, except in states where there are state laws on this subject. Again, check first with your own state officials before performing any of these modifications.

Even the simplest of tuning tricks makes a Z28 engine come alive, especially at low end on the street where stock high-performance engines are at their weakest. The most effective supertune tricks involve small but vital modifications to the ignition and carburetion systems. These changes generally fall under the heading of what most people would call a "dyno tune" (Figs. 3-1 and 3-2). While it *is* ideal to have the use of a chassis dyno to check the results of each small change as it's made, it's not absolutely necessary to have access to one to achieve satisfactory results.

IGNITION SYSTEM

From 1970 to 1974, all Z28 engines had a standard single-point Delco-Remy distributor. For 1979 and up models you'll have to deal with the General Motors HEI (High Energy Ignition) electronic system. No big sweat. Just make sure you know what distributor is on your engine before tackling it.

In either case, it's ideal to have access to a Sun distributor testing machine. If not, just use our figures. The results will be as good for all intents and purposes.

Fig. 3-1. Ideally, supertuning should be done at a facility with a chassis dyno. But short of that you can still get good results doing it yourself.

Delco-Remy Distributor

Remove the air cleaner, then the distributor (Fig. 3-3).

We put a '73 distributor on a Sun machine to find out what a

Fig. 3-2. Scopes and electronic equipment can make your tuneup extra sharp, and your car will probably run better if the operator knows what he's doing.

typical stock advance curve would be like (Fig. 3-4). The distributor had 0° at 1000 rpm, 5° at 1800, 8° at 2900 and 10° at 4200 rpm—very retarded but typical of a late model smogger distributor.

Remove and discard the RFI shields. This allows heat which builds up around the points to dissipate more rapidly. Also, crimp the holddown screws of the circuit-breaker plate assembly to prevent any unwanted movement. This assures accurate dwell settings with no changes.

Because the stock points will probably exhibit bounce about 5000 rpm on the Sun machine, replace them with Mallory Super Duty 102X points. Lastly, remove the bushing stop under the weights to allow the weights to advance to their maximum.

Remove the stock centrifugal weights and distributor springs and replace the weights with units especially ground for GM distributors by *Mr. Gasket.* Also replace the springs with lighter units. Before installing the new weights and springs, lubricate the centrifugal weight base to assure free movement of the weights as they advance (see Figs. 3-5 to 3-10).

Back on the Sun machine, advance will now start with 3 degrees at 700 rpm, then go to 6 degrees at 1400 rpm and will be totally advanced to 13 degrees at only 1900 rpm. Set dwell at 28 degrees and install the distributor back in the car. Before replacing

Fig. 3-3. First step is to remove the distributor.

Fig. 3-4. Mount the distributor in a Sun distributor testing machine and disassemble.

63

the distributor in the engine, clean the rotor top and tongue to make sure you're getting good contact. Also lube the distributor cam lobes (Figs. 3-11 to 3-15).

HEI Electronic System

Electronic ignition systems have some of the same drawbacks as their ignition-point-equipped predecessors had—the most glaring being a retarded advance curve.

The HEI system (Figs. 3-16 to 3-22) is, of course, a breakerless system. It utilizes an all-electronic module, pickup coil and timer core in place of the more conventional ignition pin points and condenser. The condenser is used here for noise suppression only. Such previously troublesome maladies as ignition-point pitting, distributor shaft wear and rubbing block wear are a thing of the past. So you won't have to worry about ignition troubles because of these factors.

Since the ignition coil is part of the HEI distributor, there's no need for a distributor-to-coil primary lead or a secondary high-voltage lead. Since this is a full 12-volt system, it does not require a resistance wire. The magnetic pickup consists of a rotating timing core attached to the distributor shaft, a stationary pole piece, a permanent magnet and a pickup coil.

When the distributor shaft rotates, the teeth of the timer core line up and pass the teeth of the pole piece, inducing voltage in the pickup coil. This, in turn, signals the all-electronic module to open the ignition coil primary circuit. Maximum inductance current is reached at the moment the timer core teeth are lined up with the teeth on the pole piece. At the instant the timer core teeth start to pass the pole teeth, the primary current decreases and a high voltage is induced in the ignition coil secondary winding. The voltage is directed through the rotor and high-voltage leads to fire the spark plugs.

The vacuum diaphragm is connected by linkage to the pole piece. When the diaphragm moves against spring pressure, it rotates the pole piece. This rotation allows the poles to advance in relation to the timer core. The timer core is rotated about the shaft by conventional advance weights, thus providing centrifugal advance. The quickness of centrifugal advance is controlled by conventional distributor advance springs.

A convenient tachometer connection is incorporated in the wiring connector on one side of the distributor. However, due to its transistorized design, the HEI system will not trigger some model tachs. So if you're thinking of switching to an HEI system, make

Fig. 3-5. At the top of the conventional Delco distributor are the distributor weights and advance springs. Run the advance curve on the Sun machine, then remove the weights and springs.

sure you have a tach that's compatible. Also, if the tach is not connected correctly to the distributor, the HEI module can blow out.

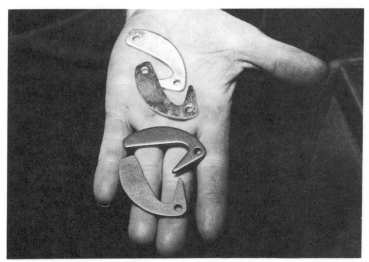

Fig. 3-6. Special centrifugal advance weights are available in any speed shop for the Delco distributor.

Fig. 3-7. Special weight on the right compared to the stock weight on the left. A slightly different shape and weight alter the advance curve.

The first thing we wanted to know was what kind of stock ignition curve the HEI typically carries from the factory. We removed the distributor assembly from a '74 L-82 engine, after loosening the distributor cover and cap. We hooked up the HEI on the Sun machine and ran up the curve. By the way, a special adapter unit must be attached to the Sun distributor machine before electronic ignition systems can be tested on it (Fig. 3-18).

The top of the electronic ignition system distributor advance springs and centrifugal weights are right up on top where they're easy to get at. Before touching anything, we dialed in the machine and we recorded the stock centrifugal advance curve. Advance began with 2 degrees at 1350 rpm. At 2000 rpm, the distributor had 6.5° advance. At 3400 rpm, there were 10° advance, and full advance was reached at 4200 rpm with 11° total. This is a typical curve for this distributor.

A good rule of thumb is that a high-performance Z28 needs full advance around 2000-2400 rpm. This gives good throttle response and brisk performance throughout an engine's rpm range. The

Fig. 3-8. Notice the difference in the thickness of the wire used on the stock advance spring (left) and the special spring (right).

exact rate of advance has to be determined in each individual instance, of course. Other factors such as compression ratio, type of transmission, rear axle gearing and weight of the car are also determining factors in where your total advance should come in. One thing you don't want to do is dial in too much advance too quickly. This simply results in pre-ignition—engine knock—which will quickly burn holes in the tops of your pistons and destroy your engine if not checked.

Another factor that must enter into the timing equation is the type of fuel used. High-octane gas will prevent engine knock even on cars with radical timing dialed into the distributor. However, on cars operating on regular gas or unleaded gas (as all '77s ended up with catalytic converters), you can't go overboard with timing or you'll find yourself walking home.

Although the HEI centrifugal advance weights have their own special little shape (Fig. 3-21), you'll quickly find that conventional

Fig. 3-9. Distributor with special weights and springs installed.

GM Delco-shaped advance weights work just as well, despite the slightly different shape. You'll also find that the previously used *Mr. Gasket* high-performance weights and springs are a bit much for this particular setup. With the *Mr. Gasket* custom weights and springs installed in the distributor, total advance will be about 18° at 2200 rpm. This would be fine for a high-compression, suitably modified street engine running on Sunoco 260. However, for a low-compression, catalytic converter-equipped Z28 Camaro, this particular setup is a no-no.

So just leave the stock weights in and simply change the advance springs. The weights essentially control the amount of advance and the springs control the *rate* of advance. Since you're already getting 11° total advance (that's 22 engine degrees), you can dial in 10° initially, giving a total of 32° advance. This is more than sufficient for a stone stock Z28. Hence, you only have to find a set of springs which allow the *rate* of advance to be quicker while maintaining the stock amount of advance.

Your final advance curve should stack up approximately like this: Centrifugal advance starts with 2° at 800 rpm. At 1050 rpm, 6° is present and 10° advance dialed in at 1850 rpm. Full advance should be 11° at 2200 rpm.

Before reinstalling the distributor in the engine, shim up the shaft and plan to .005-inch. After reinstalling the distributor in the

Fig. 3-10. Before installing special weights and springs, lightly lubricate the base.

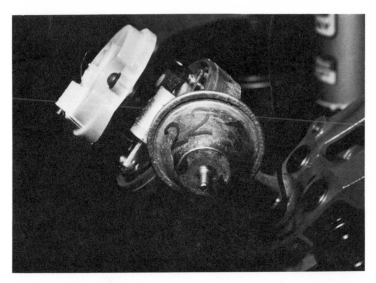

Fig. 3-11. After determining the new advance curve on the Sun machine, mark the total advance in the distributor so that you'll remember later on when setting the initial advance.

engine, block off the vacuum advance unit by plugging the hose and making it inoperative. Then dial in 11° initial advance. So now your degrees total advance (11 plus 11 plus 11; you double crank degrees to get engine degrees and then add the initial advance).

CARBURETION

One of two carburetors was used on all Z28 350 cubic inch engines. On the LT-1 engines, a Holley 4-barrel was used. On the L-82 and LM-1 engines, a Rochester quadrajet 4-barrel was used. The photos will help you to determine which carburetor you have if you're not sure (Figs. 3-23 to 3-56).

Holley 4-barrel

Remove the primary fuel bowls, after you have removed the carb from the intake manifold.

Check the jets in the primary bowls. Measure the jets with marked drill bits. Replace them with jets .003-inch richer (Figs. 3-29, 3-30 and 3-31). NOTE: The only proper way to jet a carb is on a chassis dyno where you can see the results of each jet change with an exhaust gas analyzer or on the dragstrip where you can make a run after each jet change to determine the results. We can only give you in-the-ball-park jet recommendations here, as each application may vary slightly.

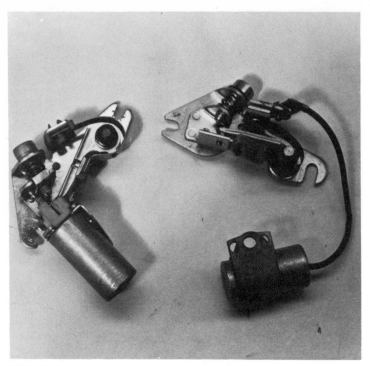

Fig. 3-12. Stock Uniset points (left) and special Mallory 102X heavy-duty springs (right).

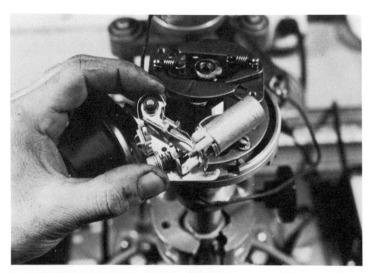

Fig. 3-13. Stock Uniset points should be removed.

Fig. 3-14. A Sun distributor testing machine is a must for this kind of work.

While the primary fuel bowl is removed, look for a fiber insert block plate. Not all Holleys have them. If your carb does have one, remove it and throw it away.

Install an anti-slosh vent tube. This is a Holley service item available in any speed shop as are jets for Holleys.

Fig. 3-15. Before final assembly, shim up the distributor shaft end play.

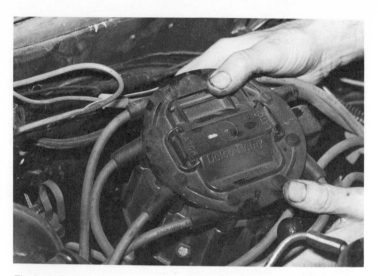

Fig. 3-16. Remove the distributor cap on the GM HEI electronic ignition.

Fig. 3-17. Remove the HEI from the engine. Notice the difference in appearance from the conventional Delco distributor.

Fig. 3-18. The HEI distributor is also tested on the Sun machine, but a special adaptor is necessary.

Remove the secondary fuel bowl. Install either No. 74 or No. 76 jets as a starting point. Install an anti-slosh vent tube on the secondary side as well.

If you're working with a very early Holley, install a .110-inch needle and seat assembly. This is also known as the window needle and seat assembly. Install them in both fuel bowls.

Remove the vacuum chamber secondary unit. Inside you'll find a spring which controls the opening of the secondary barrels. A

Fig. 3-19. Partially disassembled, the HEI looks similar to the Delco distributor. Remove the advance springs only; leave the weights in and use as is.

light spring will get your secondaries open sooner. A heavier spring will delay the opening. Again, this can only be worked out while driving the car and noticing the response of the engine. Replacement springs are a Holley service item available through

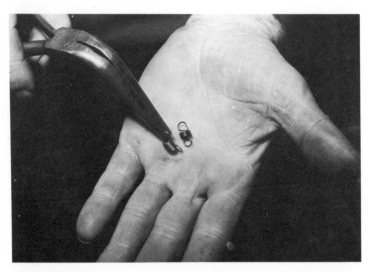

Fig. 3-20. Special springs should be substituted for the heavier stock wire springs.

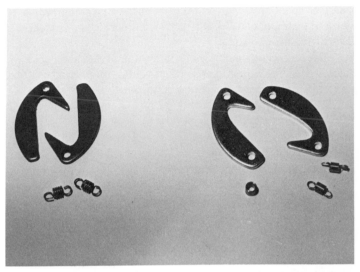

Fig. 3-21. A wide range of weights and springs is available to custom tailor an advance curve into an HEI distributor.

speed shops. A less precise way to advance the opening of the secondaries is to cut the stock spring.

Remove the screw that holds on the accelerator pump cam. Holley makes other accelerator pump cams that can replace the stock unit. If your engine idles at a high rpm, you want the air/fuel

Fig. 3-22. HEI distributor with the custom weights installed.

charge to come in later so that it's not all used up while the car is idling. If your engine idles at a more leisurely pace, you want the charge to come in sooner.

The accelerator pump shot can also be varied somewhat by turning the accelerator pump adjustment screw. Readjust this screw after you change accelerator pump cams.

Reassemble the carb.

After reinstalling the needle and seat assembly (Fig. 3-53), adjust the floats to line up with the two screws in the bowl wall. This is a rough in-the-ballpark setting that will allow you to start the engine and make a final adjustment.

During reassembly, make sure all the gaskets are the same as the original equipment gaskets (Fig. 3-49). There are some very freaky Holley gaskets floating around that may block up some vital passages.

With the float bowl plug removed, adjust the float levels until gas just begins to dribble out of the sight hole with the engine idling. If fuel sloshes out of the vent tubes under hard acceleration, longer tubes are available.

Adjust the idle mixture and idle speed screws. Top off the carb modifications with a low restriction, high-performance air cleaner.

Fig. 3-23. First step in modifying the carburetor is to remove it from the engine. You can work with only the top half of a Quadrajet removed, but it's easier and neater to remove the entire carb and work on a bench.

Fig. 3-24. Determine whether your Z28 engine has a Rochester Quadrajet or a Holley 4-barrel. This is the Rochester Quadrajet.

Fig. 3-25. After the carb is off the engine and on a bench, you can begin disassembly. If you live in a warm climate, you can cut off the choke lockout linkage and remove it completely. Leave it on if you drive in cold weather.

77

Fig. 3-26. Dissassemble the carburetor.

Rochester Quadrajet

First, unbolt the carb from the intake manifold, place it on a workbench and dismantle it. When removing the top half of the carb, be very careful not to rip the gasket so that it can be reused.

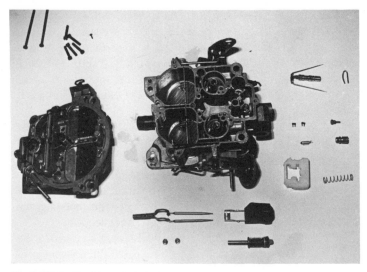

Fig. 3-27. The Rochester Quadrajet completely dissassembled.

Fig. 3-28. Be careful when removing the secondary metering rods.

Remove and measure the primary jets. On our particular engine, the orifices measured .074-inch in diameter. Normally, you would drill out jets a minimum of .003-inch when going after maximum performance. If you're after economy and performance, drill out the orifices only .002-inch (Fig. 3-48). One thousandth of an inch may not seem critical. Believe it, it *is* in the performance of your car.

Measure the secondary metering rod tips with a micrometer (Fig. 3-33). Average is .045-inch in diameter. We substituted tips with .043-inch diameter tips. A good rule of thumb is to use metering rods .002-.004-inch smaller, set the float setting to stock specs and leave the accelerator pump plunger stock rather than cut 1/8-inch off, which is normal procedure in setting up a Quadrajet. It also wreaks havoc with gas mileage.

Button up the carb and install it back on the car. Adjust the secondary air flaps after the carb is back on the car (Figs. 3-37, 3-38 and 3-39). Use a gauge to set the spring tension; this is much more precise than doing it by feel. What you want to end up with is the secondary air flap opening at around 3500 rpm under load. This gives you power when you punch it but prevents bogging and unneeded fuel from being pumped in when it's not needed.

For warm weather driving, you might want to remove the choke lockout linkage entirely. This eliminates the possibility of the lockout sticking and not allowing the secondary air flaps to

Fig. 3-29. Primary carb jets are removed and reinstalled with a regular flat tip screwdriver.

Fig. 3-30. Quadrajet primary jets look like this. They're usually too lean for peak performance in stock size.

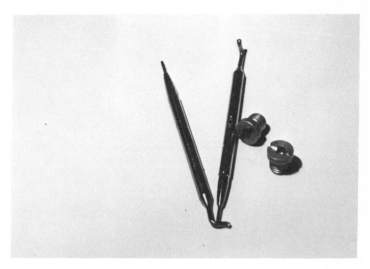

Fig. 3-31. Jets and metering rods in all sizes are available from speed shops and auto parts stores that stock Rochester parts.

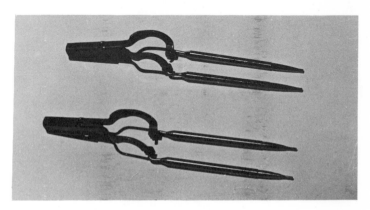

Fig. 3-32. Secondary metering rods control the amount of gas going into secondaries when you punch it.

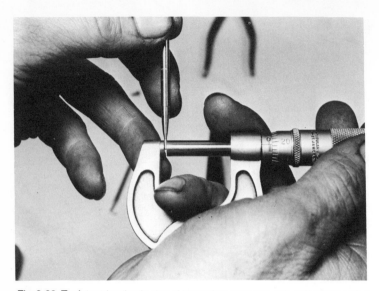

Fig. 3-33. To determine the tip size of secondary metering rods, mike them with a micrometer. You want to install new rods about .003-inch under the size of the stock rods.

Fig. 3-34. Some tuners cut about ⅛-inch off the accelerator pump plunger. This is OK for all-out performance engines.

Fig. 3-35. Simply mount the plunger in a vise and use a hacksaw to cut off ⅛-inch. We don't recommend this for mild street engines.

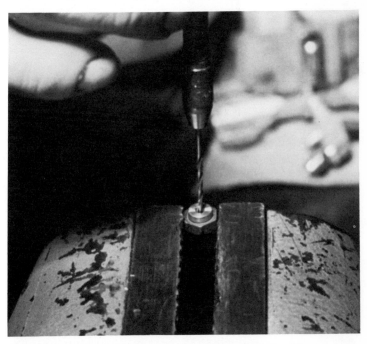

Fig. 3-36. Sometimes, larger primary jets are hard to find in the right size. In this case, *carefully* drill out the stock jets.

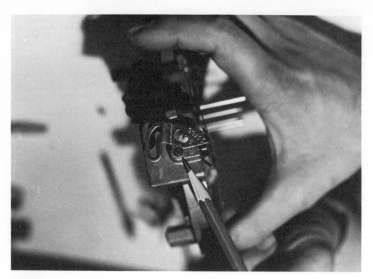

Fig. 3-37. The secondary air flaps are controlled by this screw and the Allen setscrew in Fig. 3-38.

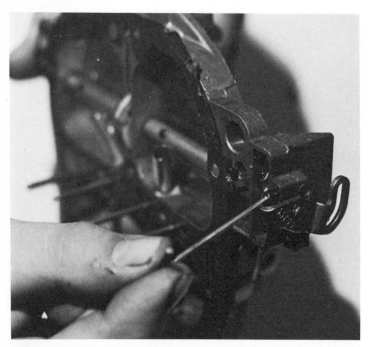

Fig. 3-38. This Allen setscrew and the screws in Fig. 3-37 control secondary air flaps.

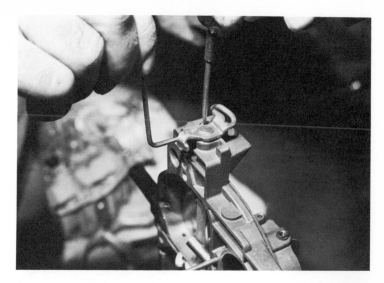

Fig. 3-39. To adjust the point at which the secondaries open, you must adjust both screws at the same time.

Fig. 3-40. To accurately measure the secondary flap opening point, use a dial indicator.

Fig. 3-41. After reassembly, adjust the fast idle cam to the desired point with the carb on the car.

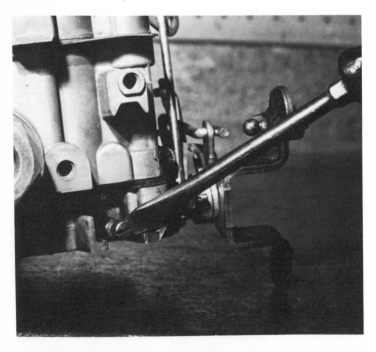

Fig. 3-42. Adjust the air-fuel mixture with this screw with the carb on the car and the engine idle set to the manufacturer's specs.

Fig. 3-43. Block off unused vacuum takeoffs to prevent surging and rough idle.

Fig. 3-44. If your engine uses a Holley 4-barrel, this is what it looks like.

Fig. 3-45. Completely disassemble the Holley carb after removing it from the engine.

Fig. 3-46. Check the size of the jets in the primary bowls. Measure the jets with marked drill bits.

Fig. 3-47. Replace them with jets .003-inch larger.

Fig. 3-48. Holley jets in all sizes are available from many sources including many speed shops. This is preferred. But if you can't obtain new jets, you can carefully drill out the stock jets to the desired size.

Fig. 3-49. Before reassembly, make sure all the gaskets are the same as original equipment and that all holes and vents are open.

open. In cold climates, however, leave the link as is. Without this link, which is part of the choke mechanism, the engine may be hard to start.

You might want to top off your supertune with a low restriction, high-performance air cleaner. Make sure you block off all the connection points to the carb if you go for a high-performance air cleaner. If they're not blocked off, you'll be getting vacuum leaks, leanness that you don't need, rough running and surging.

So what will all this supertuning net you? Generally, we've found that a sharp supertune can knock about a half second off your ET and add about 5-6 mph to your trap speeds on the strip. On the street, you'll have throttle response, something that generally

Fig. 3-50. If you're working with a very early Holley, install, a .110-inch needle and seat assembly.

Fig. 3-51. During reassembly, make sure the bolts holding on the fuel bowls are secure.

Fig. 3-52. Some tuners forget about this side bowl bolt. It must be secure.

Fig. 3-53. After reinstalling the needle and seat, adjust the floats to line up with the two screws in the bowl wall. This is a rough adjustment that will allow you to start the car and make the final adjustment with engine running.

Fig. 3-54. Remove the vacuum secondary unit screws.

Fig. 3-55. Inside the vacuum secondary, you'll find a spring that controls when the secondaries open up. Springs of different tension are available from speed shops and auto parts stores. Installing a lighter spring will give you sooner response.

Fig. 3-56. A screw holds on the accelerator pump cam. Holley makes dozens of replacement accelerator pump cams that will allow you to tailor your carb's response.

hasn't been seen on stock domestic cars since 1968. You'll probably also be getting slightly better gas mileage, since your engine is now operating more efficiently and can more fully utilize the gasoline it ingests. All around, it's not a bad deal.

Chapter 4
Factory Performance Parts For The Z28

It's common knowledge today that the Chevy small block, as found in the Z28, is one of the best performing engines ever to come out of Detroit. The engine has always developed lots of horsepower per cubic inch, even in stock form. And when modified, it's an absolute screamer. The Chevrolet small block has always produced more horsepower per cubic inch than it had any right to on paper. Credit this to the Chevrolet engineers who selected the bore, stroke, porting, valve size and camshaft combinations.

As everyone knows by now, many parts are interchangeable throughout the Chevrolet small block series (Fig. 4-1). This is a big help when building up a small block Chevy on a limited budget. The whole key of high-performance parts is as good as any speed equipment manufacturer's for the small block. The small block does have certain limitations if you're building an engine for all-out track racing. Then you must go to the speed equipment manufacturers for the real exotica. But for anything short of an all-out track engine, you can't go too far wrong by delving into the Chevrolet high-performance parts catalog (Figs. 4-2 and 4-3).

You'll find small block Chevy engines around in displacements of 265, 267, 283, 302, 305, 307, 327, 350 and 400 cubic inches. They're all basically the same engine. The various displacements were engineered by simply juggling the bore and stroke. Factory engineers never even varied the block deck height when they

Fig. 4-1. The 1967-68 302/290 engine is a good source of many high-performance Chevrolet parts that will interchange with other small-block engines.

lengthened the stroke. This means that there are interchange possibilities galore.

The parts numbers here are the latest available as of this writing. Please don't hold us responsible for any changes that might have occurred between the writing and the printing of this book.

Let's start at the top of the engine and work our way down to the lower end.

INTAKE MANIFOLDS

Chevrolet offers almost every conceivable way of getting the air/fuel mixture into the cylinders. We'll eliminate the Rochester fuel injection right here. It hasn't been offered from the factory since 1965 and is relatively difficult to keep in tune. In addition, it was valued not so much for producing additional horsepower as it was for crisp, clean throttle response. It also had benefits for road racing in that inertia forces during hard cornering and braking did not affect fuel metering. However, with such a selection of carburetors and manifolds available from the factory, there's really no need to fool around with the Rochester setup.

Fig. 4-2. Later L-82, LM-1 and LG-4 engines can be hopped up, using high-performance parts from the Chevrolet heavy-duty parts catalog.

In the Chevrolet high-performance parts manuals, you have your choice of low-rise cast iron single 4-barrel, aluminum single 4-barrel, low-rise cast iron dual 4-barrel and high-rise aluminum dual 4-barrel ram induction setups (Fig. 4-4).

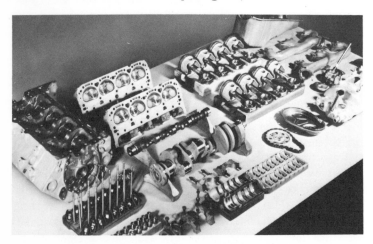

Fig. 4-3. A wide range of parts is available through any Chevrolet dealer. Use the parts numbers on these pages as an ordering guide.

Fig. 4-4. The most exotic intake combination is the Z282 and Z284 dual ram quad setup, but it's not recommended for the street.

About 90% of the time, the best combination for the street is the high-rise aluminum single 4-barrel setup. It will mount up to an 850 cfm Holley, which is all anyone would really need on a small block (Fig. 4-5). The aluminum high-rise was used on all high-

Fig. 4-5. A better choice would be a Holley 4-barrel, like this 800 cfm unit used on the early 302 engines.

performance 327 Corvette engines, the 302 Z28 engines, and on the high-performance 350 cubic inch LT-1 engines. The manifold is part number 3917610. If you can't afford a big Holley with this manifold, it will also mount any big Carter AFB carb, even to the E-series Daytona. You might want to update your later L-82 or LM-1 engine with this manifold.

Just for your information, the low-rise cast iron intake manifold used on the L-82 and LM-1 engines with the Quadrajet 4-barrel (Fig. 4-6) is part number 3958624.

If you're a multiple carburetor fan, Chevrolet has not one but *two* dual 4-barrel setups. Neither one is recommended for the street, although both have been used on the street. However, we still feel one large 4-barrel will give you all the performance you can use on the street without the tuning headaches.

If you're insistent, though, the first dual quad setup is from the old, high-performance 283 Corvette engines. It will mount two

Fig. 4-6. Late model Z28s use the Rochester Quadrajet 4-barrel. While not a real performance carb, it can be modified for better performance by following the instructions in Chapter 3.

Carter WCFB 4-barrel carburetors. These carburetors are obsolete and the manifold will not take large late model Holleys or Carter AFBs. The carburetors sit in line and look hairy as hell, though. If you're scrounging around through junk yards, look for part number 3741029. This intake manifold, by the way, is made of cast iron.

For even more performance that you can't use until you hit six grand, you can use the staggered ram dual quad intake manifold that was optional over-the-counter for the 302 Z28s. It's part number 3940077. The usual carburetion for this manifold is two 600 cfm Holleys. But some racers are running larger carbs in all-out competition applications on this manifold.

Naturally, you'll want to use the high-capacity fuel pump with any engine that you're modifying. It's part number 6415325.

As for the carburetors themselves, a good choice for most small block engines is an 800 cfm Holley 4-barrel single-pumper with 1 11/16-inch throttle bores. The Holley part number for the carburetor is R-4053A. The Chevrolet part number is 3972121.

If you're contemplating the use of the ram quad setup, you'll need two carbs which are part number 3957859. The complete assembly, including manifold, carburetors, gaskets and all nuts, bolts, springs, brackets and linkage can be ordered as a unit under part number 394007.

CAMSHAFTS

Before we discuss actual camshaft specifications, keep in mind that Chevrolet always includes clearance ramps in their valve timing specifications for hydraulic cams. The clearance ramps take up the valve lash slowly before the valve actually begins to open or close. Since this distance is quite a bit longer than the actual valve timing event, the actual valve timing is much milder than the "paper" or theoretical timing specs and is not the cam's actual valve timing.

Let's take the hydraulic cams first. Number one is the cam used on all the medium-performance engines of past years like the 327/275, 327/300, the 350/300 and the 350/270. You'd want to install this cam into a Z28 block if you were looking for economical highway cruising and the smoothest street performance. Intake duration is 310°. Exhaust duration is 320°. Overlap measures 90°. Valve lift is .390-inch intake and .410-inch exhaust. The part number is 3733431. On paper it looks like a hot cam packing plenty of duration, but in reality it's a very smooth idling cam with not much top end. Remember, those numbers are only "paper" timings.

The other hydraulic cam in Chevrolet's parts catalog *is* pretty hot. This cam is used on the old 327/350 and 350/350 Corvette engines and also on the 327/325 Chevy II engines produced a few years ago. The cam has an intake and an exhaust duration of 342° with 114° overlap and .447-inch lift. If you like a quiet hydraulic cam with plenty of punch, this part number 3863151 is it.

The solid-lifter cams vary from semi-wild to all-out wild. Chevy's first hot solid-lifter cam was used in 1956 Corvettes. Timing was 287° duration on both intake and exhaust. Lift was .404/.413 inches, intake/exhaust. If you want a cam that packs lots of midrange wallop with some top end sacrifice this is it. It's part number 3734077.

In 1957, Chevrolet changed the lift to .393-inch on intake and .399-inch on exhaust. Valve timing remained the same. This is the famed Duntov cam, or the 097 cam, that remained unchanged from 1957 to 1963. It's still used by oval track racers and some road racers today. It packs a lot of low- and midrange punch and has a very flat torque curve. The Duntov cam is part number 3736097.

In 1964, Chevy engineers wanted lots more top end power, for which they were willing to sacrifice a good deal of low and midrange performance. They designed a brand new cam which was used in 327/365 and 327/375 "fuelie" engines. The same cam was also used as the stock cam for 302 Z28s. It's a wild cam with timing of 345° intake and exhaust duration and with .488-inch lift. It's also known as the 30-across cam. That's what many racers call it because that is the valve lash setting for both the intake and exhaust. It is part number 3849346.

An even wilder cam is the optional service cam that was offered for 302 Z28s. Since it has a slightly shorter duration but a higher lift, you must make a careful check of valve-to-piston clearance. The intake duration is 333°, exhaust duration is 346°, overlap is 118° and lift is .492-inch. This one is part number 3927140.

In 1970, Chevy wanted to make the LT-1 350 engine a little more "streetable." They thought the engine with the 30-across cam was just too lumpy, except for diehard enthusiasts who wouldn't have anything milder in their engine. So they designed a slightly milder cam for the engine that idled a little smoother, had more low end torque and still had plenty of top end punch. This cam has 317° intake duration, 346° exhaust duration, .458- inch intake lift, .484-inch exhaust lift and 96° overlap. It's the stock cam in all 1970-72 Z28 engines. It is part number 3972182.

A few years ago, there were rumors of a super-duper Chevrolet cam that was offered in '65½ fuel injection engines supposedly built for road racing by the factory. It was supposed to have 534° duration. To clear up the mystery, we checked with Chevrolet's top camshaft engineer, Bill Howell. Howell told us that he, too, was fascinated by the stories and did some research for us. He learned that someone had read a blueprint for the 30-across cam without subtracting the clearance ramps from the total timing event. Another bit of evidence to bear this out is that the mystery cam was supposed to have had .488-inch lift—the same spec as the 30-across cam. Lay one more mystery to rest.

For all these cams, you should use the good valve springs, part number 3927142. In most cases, these valve springs should be installed at a height of 1.70-inch. The good retainers are part number 3729363 and the valve locks are part number 3838029. The heavy-duty mechanical valve lifter that should be employed bears part number 5231285. The heavy-duty hydraulic lifter is part number 3799644.

Production high-performance pushrods, part number 3796243, have a hardened steel tip inserted into one end and should be installed with the inserted end up against the rocker arm. The high-performance rocker arms, part number 3843359, have a polished pallet to minimize friction and can be easily identified by a raised letter "O" forged into the pallet end of the rocker.

CYLINDER HEADS

As is the case with camshafts, all cylinder heads throughout the small block Chevy series are interchangeable. That is, any cylinder head will bolt onto any block. Naturally, if you're using a late cylinder head with big parts, you'd want to match the intake manifold and use one also with big ports.

Chevy has made eight different cylinder heads for the small block engine. Each differs in port and/or valve size and combustion chamber volume. Chevy made both low and high-compression heads for the 265 block, but they are of no interest to us here.

The first good head popped up in 1957. It's the 283 high-compression head which has good combustion chamber design and spark plug cooling. Valves are a rather small—1.72 inches on intake and 1.50 inches on exhaust. The current part number for this head is 3928454, in case you run into a set in a salvage yard. The earlier part number for this same cylinder head is 3817682.

The next most interesting heads in the Chevrolet catalog were the 1960 Corvette units, which were cast in aluminum. These heads, besides being lighter, had larger parts and valves. Intake valve size was brought out to 1.94 inches. They were discontinued because of casting problems which cropped up in this early attempt to fabricate aluminum parts. They are rare birds with no available part number.

The following year, 1961, Chevrolet brought out the identical big port, big valve head (Fig. 4-7). However, it was cast in iron instead of aluminum. These heads were used until 1964 on the high-performance engines and are still in use today on 1977-present LM-1 Z28 engines. The current part number is 3928494. The earlier part number is 3817681.

In 1964, when Chevrolet engineers were modifying the small block for much more power, they designed a new set of cylinder heads. They were used from 1964 through 1970 on all the high-performance Chevrolet small block engines. These heads can be found on the 327/350, 350/350, 302 Z28 engines and 327/325 Chevy II engines. They have modified combustion chambers, even larger ports and 2.02-inch intake valves with 1.60-inch exhaust

Fig. 4-7. Chevy high-performance angle-plug heads feature large valve sizes. Notice the angle of the spark plugs for better flame travel in the combustion chamber.

valves. These heads, also known as fuelie heads, are part number 3928455. An earlier part number for this same cylinder head is 3853608.

With the introduction of the LT-1 high-performance engine for the Corvette and 350 Z28 Camaro in 1970, a new head was used and has been used since then on *all* L-82 engines. This head uses a screw-in rocker arm stud rather than the pressed-in stud used previously. Heads that have been drilled and tapped for the screw-in studs (Fig. 4-8) are part number 3987376. This LT-1 head has identical ports and valves as the '64-70 high-performance head. Only the method of attaching the stud differs. By the way, any earlier head can be tapped to accept the screw-in studs. And it might also be helpful to know that any small block Chevy head can be used on either side of the engine.

In 1971, Chevrolet engineers designed another variation of the small block high-performance cylinder head and offered the new design as a service package over-the-counter item only. The new cylinder head has not been installed as standard equipment on any production engine. Again, valves and ports are the same as the '64 high-performance and LT-1 cylinder head (Fig. 4-9). However, the spark plug holes are angled to give better flame travel in the combustion chamber and much more efficient combustion, thereby producing more horsepower. The angle plug heads (Fig. 4-7) have part number 3965742.

With any of the late high-performance cylinder heads, the best intake valve is part number 3849814. This is a swirl-polished alloy steel valve with 2.023-inch head diameter. The best 1.605-inch exhaust valve, also made of alloy steel with aluminized face has part number 3849818.

Screw-in rocker arm studs, part number 3973416, are designed to be used with hardened steel guide plates, part number 3973418, to control the side movement of the pushrods. Use stainless steel head gasket, part number 3916336, for all high-performance applications. Also, see Figs. 4-10 and 4-11.

EXHAUST MANIFOLDS

There's not really much worth mentioning in the way of factory high-performance exhaust manifolds. Chevy has never really gone in much for cast iron factory headers the way Pontiac and Ford have. They assumed that most racers would swap for steel tube headers anyway.

Fig. 4-8. All late model Z28 heads have screw-in studs for better reliability at high rpm.

For a really budget build-up, in case you can't afford tube headers, look for the large capacity high-performance Corvette exhaust manifolds. They're called "ram's horn" pipes because that's what they look like. They've been used on all 327 and 350-cubic inch high-performance engines, plus the 302 Z28s. These manifolds dump into huge 2.5-inch head pipes so you obtain good flow (Fig. 4-12). The right side is part number 3814970 and the left, part number 3846563.

Fig. 4-9. Large intake ports of the nagle plug head are evident here. LT-1 heads have the same port sizes.

Fig. 4-10. Large exhaust ports help scavenge exhaust gases at high rpm.

Available over-the-counter in '67 and '68 for 302 Z28s was a set of real tubing headers made for Chevrolet by an independent header manufacturer. These units carried a factory part number and, from what we've learned, can still be ordered over your dealer's parts counter. The right side is part number 3916384. The left side is part number 3916383.

BLOCKS, CRANKS

There are two basic cylinder blocks that are ideal for high-performance engines. One is the block used for 350 LT-1, 302 Z28 and high-performance 327 engines. This block has a 4.00-inch bore size. The other block is used only on the 400-cubic inch LF-6 small block engines and has a bore size of 4.125 inches. Both have 4-bolt main bearing caps. Many dealers insist that there are no part numbers for bare Chevrolet blocks. Nonsense. The 4.00-inch bore

Fig. 4-11. 302/290 heads feature large valves and ports but weaker press-in studs.

block is part number 3970015. The 4.125-inch block is part number 3951510.

While we're on the subject of blocks, some of the following information may be helpful. The 400 cubic inch small block is a low-performance engine, which uses a hydraulic cam and a 3.75-inch stroke cast iron crankshaft. The engine can be obtained in short block form under part number 3977677.

Complete engines are, of course, available from the factory. They come completely assembled but minus a few parts. In the case of the small block series, you can't do much better than the 1970 Corvette 350/370 LT-1 engine. The engine has high-compression forged pistons, 4-bolt mains, a solid-lifter cam and uses a large Holley carburetor on a high-rise aluminum intake manifold. The complete engine is part number 3972115.

A complete, crated engine from Chevrolet comes with intake and exhaust manifold, clutch, flywheel, bellhousing, distributor and water pump. It does not include the starter, alternator, carburetor or fuel pump. The same engine in short block form— that is, assembled block, crankshaft, rods, pistons and camshaft— is part number 3966921.

The crankshafts for all of Chevrolet's small block performance engines are made of forged steel and all are Tufftrided for added durability. Small block cranks produced in 1968 and later have 2.450-inch main bearing journals. Cranks prior to '68 have smaller

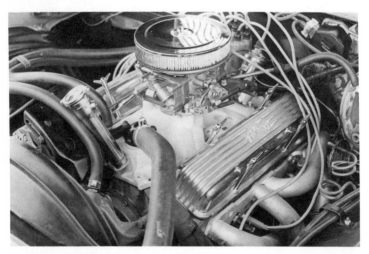

Fig. 4-12. Big single 4-barrel, tube exhaust headers, and other special components can make a real screamer out of any small block Chevy engine.

2.300-inch journals. The only exception is the 400 cubic inch engine, which alone uses a cast crank with larger 2.650-inch mains. This limits the 400 cubic inch engine to the one factory crank or to a custom crank such as those produced by custom crank grinders.

Cranks for the 350 cubic inch block are of the 2.450-inch variety. The 3.48-inch stroke crank for the 350 has part number 3941184. Since 327's were produced both before and after 1968, there are two high-performance cranks available. One has 2.450-inch mains for the newer blocks, while the other has the smaller 2.300-inch mains for the older blocks. The large journal crank is part number 3914681. The small journal crank is part number 3838495.

The same situation holds true for the high-performance 302 Z28 engines. The large journal crank has part number 3923278. The small journal crank is part number 3917265.

By the way, the earlier 283 and 265 cubic inch engines also used cranks with a 3.00-inch stroke, along with the small main bearing journals. If by any chance you're building a 265 or 283, you can use high-performance crank part number 3917265.

With any of these setups, use the 8-inch diameter heavy-duty harmonic damper, part number 3817173.

RODS, PISTONS

All Chevrolet connecting rods for high-performance small block engines are basically the same and all are interchangeable, having a center-to-center length of 5.703 inches. They are available, however, with either floating or pressed-in piston pins. In either version, they are specially selected rods that have been shotpeened and heat treated. Rods with floating pins, as used in the '69 302-cubic inch Z28, have part number 3946841. Rods with pressed-in pins have part number 3923282. Special replacement 3-inch rod nuts and bolts carry part numbers 3916399 and 3866766, respectively.

Since all small blocks, except the 400 incher, use the same length connecting rods, the pin location in the piston must be altered to compensate for the different crankshaft strokes.

All high-performance pistons used by Chevy are forged by TRW (Fig. 4-13). Pistons designed for use with the large valve heads have a compression ratio in the area of 11.0 to 1, except for '71 and '72 pistons which deal a compression ratio of about 9.0 to 1. All are available in a wide range of bore sizes from standard to .060-inch oversize.

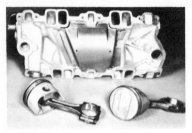

Fig. 4-13. Aluminum high-rise intake manifold and forged aluminum pistons are available from Chevrolet and will fit any Z28 engine.

For use with the 3.25-inch stroke 327 crank, the only factory pistons available used pressed pins. These pistons are part number 3871208.

Pistons for use with the 3.00-inch stroke 302 crank are available in both pressed and floating pin styles. For use on the pressed pin rods order part number 3927177. For floating pins, get part number 3946876.

Since all of the above are the standard 4-inch bore size, all can use the same piston rings. Chevrolet recommends ring set part number 3892364 for all unblown, gasoline burning, high-performance applications.

MISCELLANEOUS

A transistor ignition unit containing the coil assembly, amplifier, and harnesses is available under part number 3921048. A special distributor for use with the transistor unit carries part number 1111267.

Should you want something a little less exotic in the ignition department, Chevrolet has other high-performance distributors available. For any 302, 327 or 350 cubic inch high-performance engine, use the high tower distributor. The normal high tower distributor is part number 1111069.

For lubrication, use oil pump part number 3848907. This is the unit used on the Z28, all-solid-lifter 327 and 350 engines, all dual 4-barrel 409s and the rare '63, Z11 427. Actually, the only difference between this oil pump and the ones utilized on any small block Chevy engine is the pressure-regulated valve spring. The spring, part number 3848911, can be purchased separately and installed in any low-performance oil pump. The correct spring has 21 coils and is marked with a white paint stripe.

Chapter 5
Race Prepping
The Z28 Engine

The specifications in this chapter are intended to aid anyone preparing Chevrolet small block engines for service in competition. Basic engine specifications apply for road, oval track, or drag racing. Due to the large variety of induction and oiling systems available for different forms of competition, only the basic production system will be covered in detail. The specifications listed are intended as suggestions only. However, all are competition-proven by major competitors using these engines.

Preparation may be started with a complete engine assembly or partial engine assembly. Fitted and bare engine blocks are also available through Chevrolet Parts and Service, and appropriate service part numbers are listed.

The 1968-69 302 and 1970-72 350 cubic inch RPO Z-28 and LT-1 engines are the best high-performance designs (Fig. 5-1) featuring: 4-bolt main bearing caps, forged high-compression pistons for 4-inch bore, 3- and 3.48-inch stroke specially heat-treated crankshafts with 8-inch harmonic balancers, selected high-quality connecting rods, large port cylinder heads with 2.02-inch diameter inlet valves and 1.6-inch diameter exhaust valves, aluminum tuned runner design inlet manifold, 800 CFM Holley 4-barrel carburetor, special oil pan baffling, deep groove belt pulleys, and a mechanical lifter camshaft with special push rods and rocker arms. (1971 and '72 engines have a 9.0 to 1 compression ratio with both piston and cylinder heads revised to reduce the compression ratio.)

BASIC INTERCHANGEABILITY OF THE SMALL BLOCK SERIES

Since 1968, when all small displacement engines were brought to a common main and connecting rod journal size (2.45- and 2.1-inch respectively), there has been a basic interchangeability in components that allows building of five engine displacements out of two blocks and three crankshafts. They are as follows:

283	3 7/8-inch bore	3-inch stroke
307	3 7/8-inch bore	3 1/4-inch stroke
302	4-inch bore	3-inch stroke
327	4-inch bore	3 1/4-inch stroke
350	4-inch bore	3.48-inch stroke

In 1969, the 4-inch bore block was updated to incorporate 4-bolt main bearing caps and increased thickness main bearing webs. The 4-bolt caps were retained in all 302s and 350s until 1971, at which time the low-compression passenger car 2-barrel and 4-barrel carbureted engines were released with 2-bolt main caps again. The Z28 Camaro 350 CID truck and Corvette LT-1 still are manufactured with 4-bolt main caps. The 3 7/8-inch bore 283 and 307 blocks were never changed to accommodate 4-bolt main caps and do not have the extra cast iron in the main bearing webs that the 4-inch bore blocks do.

THE 400 CUBIC INCH SMALL BLOCK

In 1970, a 4 1/8-inch bore block was introduced in regular production as a 2-barrel carbureted regular fuel engine at 400 cubic inch displacement. This block features siamesed cylinder bores (no cooling water between bores), 4-bolt main bearing caps, and an increase in main bearing diameter to 2.65-inches. It also uses a

Fig. 5-1. Z28 Camaros have always done well in competition. But special preparation is required.

nodular iron crankshaft and 5.565-inch length connecting rod (vs. a 5.7-inch for all other small block engines). In 1973, the engine was changed to a 2-bolt main bearing cap design.

Because of the potential for larger displacements and new bore/stroke ratios from the 400 cubic inch block, a great deal of interest has been shown by engine builders in using it. There are *no* higher-performance parts available from Chevrolet for this engine. However, Chevrolet has sold a number of raw and semi-finished crankshafts to major crankshaft regrinders, which can be finished to go into the 400 block main bearings. These are primarily available in stroke lengths around 3.5-inches. In addition, some major engine bearing manufacturers have begun to make thicker shell main bearings which will allow installation of any 2.45-inch diameter main journal crank in the 2.65-inch diameter 400 block.

Camshafts, cylinder heads, intake manifolds and most other small block high-performance equipment is interchangeable with this engine. Engine displacements with various bore/stroke combinations in the 4 1/8-inch bore block are as follows:

4.126 bore, 3.00 stroke—322 CID

4.126 bore, 3.25 stroke—348 CID

4.126 bore, 3.40 stroke—365 CID spl. crank

4.126 bore, 3.48 stroke—373 CID

4.156 bore, 3.48 stroke—378 CID .030 overbore

In the event you should build a high-performance engine using the 4 1/8-inch bore block, the following cautions should be observed:

1. The engine, at 3.75-inch stroke, is externally balanced in production with an unbalanced torsional damper and flywheel. These parts or similarly unbalanced parts may be necessary to achieve final engine balance.

2. Bore distortion adjacent to the head bolts can be minimized by honing the bores with a deck plate installed on the block and bolts torqued into the head bolt holes.

3. Because of the siamesed cylinder bores, steam holes are drilled through the cylinder block deck between cylinders above and below the siamesed joint. For good cooling water circulation, and to relieve steam and air pockets, it is necessary that these holes be matched with similar holes in the head gasket and cylinder heads.

4. To prevent head gasket overhanging into the cylinder bore, the production (or any other large bore) head gasket must be used. Currently the most satisfactory head gasket for high-performance application is the Chevrolet gasket, part number 3997790. Apply aluminum paint to both sides of the gasket and allow to dry before installing. Retorque all head bolts after initial engine warmup.

The 4 1/8-inch bore block is available as a bare block from Chevrolet Parts and Service under part number 3951510.

Recommended Clearances

Piston to bore (Chevrolet forged pistons): .0055-.0065-inch measured at the centerline of the wrist pin hole, perpendicular to the pin. Finish bores with No. 500 grit stones or equivalent (smooth).

Piston ring: Minimum end clearance—top, .022-inch; second, .016-inch; oil, .016-inch.

Wrist pin: .0004-.00008-inch in the piston (.0005-.0007-inch in red for floating pin; 0-.005-inch end play preferred).

Rod bearing: .002-.0025-inch side clearance, .010-.020-inch.

Main bearing: .002-.003-inch minimum preferred; .005-.007-inch end play.

Piston to top of block (deck height): .012-.015-inch average below the deck. No part of a piston except the dome is to be higher than the deck of the block. The deck height specified is for a .020-inch steel head gasket. If a thicker head gasket is used, a piston-to-cylinder head clearance of 0.35-inch should be considered minimum.

Valve lash: .030-inch intake, .030-inch exhaust, for production cam, part number 3849346; .022-inch intake, .024-inch exhaust for optional service camshafts, part numbers 3927140 and 3965754; .024-inch intake, .030-inch exhaust for 1970 production cam, part number 3972178.

Valve-to-piston clearance: .020-inch exhaust, .015-inch intake at 0 valve lash; *note;* these are to be considered absolute minimum clearances for an engine to run below the valve train limiting speed of 7600 rpm; if you intend to run up to valve train limiting speed, more clearance should be allowed; it is common practice to allow .100-inch intake and .125-inch exhaust valve clearances for engines used in drag racing.

Reconditioning specifications

Connecting rod bearing bore diameter: 2.2247 to 2.2252 inch
Main bearing bore diameter: 2.6406 to 2.6415 inch

The recommended bolt torque and lubrication specifications for small block V-8 engines are listed in Table 1-1.

CYLINDER BLOCK

Whether starting with a new or used cylinder block, the basic requirements are that it be clean, crack-free, with reasonably straight, round cylinder bores; reasonably aligned, round main bearing bores; and main caps that fit tightly into their notches machined into the block.

The basic preparations to be performed on the block are: cleaning, boring (if required) and honing, decking (to establish the piston-top-to-cylinder-head clearance); and checking of the main bearing bores for out-of-round condition and alignment from one end of the block to the other.

Beyond the basic preparations, many engine builders perform additional operations limited only by time and money to insure the block is perfect in all dimensions. These include special acid cleaning processes to get rid of core sand, painting of the block inside and out, bottom tapping and thread chasing of all tapped holes, machining of all extraneous casting projections for reduced weight, sonic testing of cylinder walls to determine that they are of uniform thickness; magnaflux testing for crack detection, replacing the main bearing and head bolts with studs; and chamferring all tapped bolt holes and deburring all surfaces and edges. We will attempt to sort through these procedures to explain the vital operations beyond the minimum that your time and money permit.

1. *Checking of original dimensions to determine required machining:* Check the bore sizes to determine how much needs to be bored or honed to give you the required finished piston-to-bore clearance.

Check the main bores for roundness and size. Chevrolet blueprint tolerances for the main bearing bore diameter are 2.4906 to 2.4915 inches for 2.3-inch journal diameter, 2.6406 to 2.6415 inches for 2.45-inch journal crankshaft, and 2.8406 to 2.8415 inches for the 4 1/8-inch bore 400 block. If your block has main bearing bores within the tolerance shown, it will have adequate bearing crush and should perform satisfactorily. If a straight crankshaft will spin freely in the new main bearings of .002-.0025-inch clearance, it does not need to be align bored.

The main bearing saddles can also be checked for alignment using a machinists straight edge and a .0015-inch feeler gauge. With the straightedge in place you should not be able to insert or remove a .0015 feeler at any main bearing bore. The block should not be align bored unless it is necessary.

To determine how much material must be removed from the cylinder block deck surfaces, you must have the pistons, rods and crank installed that you intend to run or use accurate dimensions from them. You can actually assemble all the parts into the block and measure how far the piston is below the deck or you can measure all the dimensions with proper micrometers, etc., to arrive at the final figure.

The final dimension you want is how much must be machined from the deck surfaces to give a clearance of .035-.040 inch between the piston top (not the dome) and the cylinder head of the completed engine. The compressed thickness of the head gasket of the type being used must also be included in this calculation.

Table 5-1. Recommended bolt torque and lubricant specifications for 400 cubic inch small block V-8 engines.

		Torque	Lubricant
Main bearing		inner 70 lb./ft.	Molykote
		outer 65	Molykote
Connecting rod bolt (⅜ inch)		45-50 lb./ft. (.006-inch stretch preferred)	oil
Cylinder head bolt		65 lb./ft.	Sealant
Rocker arm stud (late HP head)		50 lb./ft.	sealant
Camshaft sprocket		20 lb./ft.	oil
Intake manifold		25 lb./ft.	oil
Flywheel		60 lb./ft.	oil
Spark plugs (conventional gasket)		25 lb./ft.	dry
Spark plugs (tapered seat)		15 lb./ft.	dry
Exhaust manifold		25 lb./ft	antisieze
Oil pan bolt		165 lb./in.	oil
Front cover bolt		75 lb./in.	oil
Rocker cover		25 lb./in.	oil
Valve lash (hot):	**Camshaft**		
	3927140	.022I	.024E
	3849346	.030I	.030E
	3972178	.024I	.030E
	3965154	.022I	.024E

Keep in mind that if you machine any appreciable amount from the block decks or heads, you also need to machine your intake manifold to restore gasket spaces and port alignment.

2. *Boring and Honing:* If you are contemplating boring a 4-inch bore small block more than .020 inch, you should attempt to find a place to get the cylinder bores sonic tested for thickness. The cylinder liners are thinner between adjacent bores to allow water flow between cylinders.

If any core shift has occurred during the casting of the block, when accompanied with an overbore, the block may crack between bores. Sonic testing is quite accurate at detecting this and the cost is reasonable if there is a tester located in your area. Look in the Yellow Pages under Testing Laboratories.

The block should be bored and honed with main bearing caps torqued in place and a deck plate installed on the head surface to reproduce the stresses normally supplied by the head bolts. Hone for final piston clearance (.005-.0055 inch for Chevrolet pistons) with a medium grit stone, establishing a good crosshatch pattern in the bore. Finish-hone with a stone of approximately 400-500 grit to give a very smooth bore finish. Present-day piston rings are lapped during their manufacture and no longer require a rough bore for good seating. On rebuilds, bores should not be rehoned unless absolutely necessary if maximum power is to be achieved from minimum ring friction. If available, honing by an automatic honing machine such as the Sunnen CK-10 is preferred.

A note regarding the use of deck plates for honing is in order here: Deck plates were invented by engine builders who demanded perfectly straight round bores after their cylinder heads were installed. There are professional engine builders who feel this is necessary for good ring sealing, since modern rings conform very well, and their experience bears them out. Chevrolet feels that use of the deck plate is preferable—and mandatory in the case of 4 1/8-inch bore block, which should always be honed with a plate if possible.

3. *Cleaning:* After all machining operations, the block should be thoroughly cleaned. Remove all oil gallery plugs and camshaft bearings. (If new cam bearings are removed carefully, they may be reused). Deburr the block with a small hand grinder and rotary file or sandpaper cones. How much time is spent here depends strictly on how important you feel it is to have a smooth block without sharp corners. Try at least to break the sharp edges remaining after the block was decked, so it can be handled without cutting your hands.

Try also to enlarge and smooth the oil drain back areas in the valve filter valley. If the block was decked, chamfer the head bolt holes with a counterbore or similar tool.

Clean all oil passages with solvent, using a rifle or other stiff bristle brush. Clean bores with hot soap and water and coat with oil immediately to prevent rust.

At this time, the block can be painted on the inside, if you prefer, using Rustoleum or Glyptal made by General Electric. Replace oil gallery plugs and cam bearings. You may also want to positively retain all welch plugs with small self-tapping screws or drive pins to be sure they won't come out unexpectedly later.

CYLINDER HEAD NO.

There are three different cylinder head assemblies available as heavy-duty service parts for the small block V-8 engine. Common features are combustion chamber volume and valve seat machining for 2.02-inch diameter inlet valves and 1.60-inch diameter exhaust valves. The cylinder head assembly consists of a cylinder head, screw-in rocker arm studs and push-rod guide plates.

Cylinder Head Assembly	Cylinder Head Casting	Usage
3987376	3991492	Service Replacement Part
336746	3991492	Off-Road racing
3965784	340292	Off-Road racing

Cylinder Head Assembly No. 3987376

This cylinder head is the standard service replacement part for 302 cubic inch (1967-1969), 327 cubic inch (1964-68), 350 cubic inch (1969-70) production high-performance engines built with a 10.0-11.1:1 compression ratio.

The spark plug machining is conventional and requires a 14mm 3/8 reach flat seat spark plug with washer.

Cylinder Head Assembly No. 336746

Experimental engine development work in late 1970 indicated that a significant horsepower improvement could be achieved by relocating the spark plug in the combustion chamber of the basic No. 3991492 cylinder head. The location was moved to place the

116

spark plug tip higher in the chamber (near the roof) and closer to the exhaust valve. Subsequent testing showed a consistent 10-12 horsepower improvement over the entire rpm range. The relocated spark plug machining requires a 14mm tapered seat spark plug.

This cylinder head assembly, part number 3965742, commonly referred to as the angled plug head, was released as a heavy-duty service part.

In 1972, a new heavy-duty service valve spring assembly, part number 330585, and valve spring cap, part number 330586, were released for the small block V-8 engine. To complement the new valve spring assembly, machining changes were required on the cylinder head. The valve guide diameter was reduced from 0.760 to 0.740 inch, and the valve spring pocket diameter was increased from 1.28 inches to 1.44 inches. Part number 336746 was assigned to the cylinder head assembly and released to replace cylinder head assembly part number 3965742 for off-road usage only.

The No. 3991492 cylinder head casting was used for cylinder head assembly part number 3965742 and is still used for cylinder head assembly part number 336746.

Cylinder Head Assembly No. 3965784

Laminar air flow studies and continuous dynamometer development work provided guidelines for an improved performance cylinder head, feasible within production casting and machining limitations. In 1973, cylinder head assembly part number 3965784 (cylinder head part number 340292) was released as a heavy-duty service part for off-road usage.

An inlet port with greater air flow capacity as cast was incorporated into the new cylinder head. Several compromises were required to include this port. The deck thickness beneath the inlet runners was reduced locally 0.060 inch (from .26 to .20) to maintain adequate core strength in the lower water jacket core. To facilitate machining the inlet manifold flange, the divider between the inlet port runners was cast 0.24-inch thick instead of the desired 0.18-inch wall thickness.

RECOMMENDED MODIFICATIONS FOR CYLINDER HEAD NO. 3965784 (CASTING NO. 340292)

The cylinder head is the key to the ultimate performance potential of the small block V-8 engine. Thorough preparation and correct modifications cannot be overemphasized.

As mentioned previously, the design features that benefit total cylinder head performance were incorporated into this cylinder head within the confines of production casting techniques and machining limitations. Modifications can be made in certain areas to achieve the maximum performance capabilities of the basic cylinder head.

Professional cylinder head porting services are available that have done extensive research into the theory and practical application of port air flow. Their knowledge is based on actual laminar air flow studies performed, using various port configurations, valve sizes and seats. Sectioned castings are normally used for these tests. This method insures that the port modifications have not left thin walls that would create durability problems. Grinding errors can be corrected in flow models, but in an actual casting a slip of the grinder usually means scrap the cylinder head or at least the inability to achieve maximum air flow from a port.

The professional cylinder head grinders have accumulated empirical knowledge in the field to substantiate the air flow improvements and individual changes they make in the basic cylinder head to improve performance. Different applications, drag racing, stock car racing versus road racing, call for special techniques in valve seating, porting, combustion chamber volume, valve spring setups, etc.

The amount of research and intensity among the many professionals involved in the porting business creates an ever-changing "state of the air" in competition cylinder head technology. Care should be exercised by the performance enthusiast in pursuing cylinder head rework to differentiate between the cosmetic features and the actual modifications that improve performance. Regarding the degree of cylinder head preparation for a specific application, a reasonable approach is essential to determine the extent of the required modifications versus the necessary financial investment to achieve this end.

The following general information is provided regarding the rework and modification of cylinder head No. 340292. Basic areas of concern are inlet and exhaust ports, inlet, exhaust valve seats, combustion chamber and valve spring pockets.

Inlet Port

The inlet port needs little modification to achieve improvements in air flow. The basic casting increases the critical cross section of the port and provides good port shape. Compromises

Fig. 5-2. Drag racing has been a forte of the Z28. Here a '69 Z28 set up for pro stock competition does a burnout to warm up the tires.

have been made in the area adjacent to the push-rod centerline, the inlet port divider and the valve seat area to permit usage of production tools. These areas can be easily modified.

With reference to the inlet port cylinder head No. 340292 the push rod in the stock position with required clearance allows a cast 1.0-inch wide port opening. By removing material from the outer wall and the divider between inlet ports, a 1.18-inch width can be obtained with adequate wall thickness. This develops a 2.30 square inch cross sectional area. Additional rework should provide a minimum cross sectional area of 2.0 square inches located 2.0 inches from the inlet flange and an area of 2.10 square inches located 2.5 inches from the inlet flange. A smaller cross sectional area at the push-rod centerline could benefit durability (thicker walls) and maintain port velocity for smaller displacement engines. Once the port cross section at 1.0 inch is opened to about 2.0 square inches, the air flow is not improved by increasing this area until further work is done in the port between the 1.0-inch line and the valve seat throat area.

The central bolt boss column between inlet ports has a thin cast wall column—0.10 inch, but the port can be widened. Material can be removed from the common wall to make it tangent to the bowl radius.

When working in the area adjacent to the highest point of the floor, care should be taken not to lower the floor, but remove material to achieve the squareness with minimum corner radius. The resulting port floor should be parallel to the cylinder head face.

Valve seating techniques are both critical and controversial. For the narrow valve seat, blend the mouth of the port close to the back side of the valve seat with straight line conical elements complemented by a gradual blending from the flat floor and walls on the short side of the port with the largest radius possible. Wide seats of 0.08-inch width offer better durability features and should be used with 60° and 90° angles, both 0.10-inch minimum width. These dimensions may be difficult to achieve in certain castings because of core shift.

The inlet valve unshrouding cutter has been changed in diameter from 2.40- to 2.34-inch diameter to reduce chamber volume and bore overhang, and to increase chamber wall thickness. This reduction does not affect air flow.

Exhaust Port

The exhaust port can be improved by correct shaping and valve seating. The exhaust gases must approach the seal smoothly and flow through the throat without becoming turbulent. Grind to form a venturi behind the valve seat with a 1.35-inch diameter throat and a cross sectional radius profile of 0.40 inch. The portion of the exhaust port adjacent to the inlet port requires more metal removed because of the cast port shape which provides water between the inlet and exhaust port. Caution must be exercised to prevent a thin wall in this area.

The back wall of the port (the long side) needs to be blended from the seat to the guide with a 2.0-inch radius. This will provide a reference surface for blending the short side (0.40-inch radius) profile into the port floor with the 1.35-inch diameter throat.

The exhaust port flange can be made to fit a particular header system or left with intentional mismatch for reverse flow check (exhaust port flange smaller than the header flange). The size and shape of the flange (even stock) has little effect on total flow.

The combustion chamber wall gets tight relative to the exhaust valve seat and can be improved by radiusing adjacent to the valve. Do not lower the approach area to the valve seat, as the flow depends on a smooth approach to the seat, and nicks or irregularities will hurt the flow.

Combustion Chamber

During rework, care should be exercised to remove a minimum amount of metal from the interior combustion chamber surfaces. Prior to any modifications, the chamber volume with valves nominally seated and the spark plug installed will average 66 cubic centimeters. This volume can be decreased by milling the cylinder head gasket surface. The volume should decrease by 0.15 cubic centimeters per 0.001-inch stock removed from the surface.

As previously mentioned, the cast deck thickness beneath the inlet port runners was reduced locally from 0.26 inch to 0.20 inch. A very minimum of stock should be removed from the gasket surface, normally only as required for squareness. An absolute maximum for removal would be 0.030 inch.

When metal is removed from the cylinder head gasket surface, machining may be required on the inlet manifold bottom and side surfaces to insure proper attaching bolt and inlet port flange alignment. Table 5-2 lists metal removal quantities.

Valve Spring Pockets

Provisions have been made to accommodate valve springs with increased diameter and installed height. The corner radius or chamfer of the tool used to enlarge the pocket is very critical and must be maintained to prevent a stress riser.

Crankshaft

Remove any burrs from oil holes and passages and polish journals with No. 400 sandpaper.

Magnaflux inspection may show small heat-treat cracks around oil holes. These are not detrimental as long as they do not extend into the journal fillet radii. Manufacturing specifications allow a certain amount of main journal runout (or bend) in the finished crankshaft. It is not possible to straighten these crankshafts in a hydraulic press without cracking them; however, several reputable crankshaft specialty shops can straighten them by a peening process if a perfectly true crankshaft is desired.

All production 302 and heavy-duty 327 and 350 crankshafts are "Tufftride" heat treated to improve journal hardness and give greater fatigue strength for high-performance durability. This feature is an improvement to any high-performance forged crankshaft and should be included in any engine build. Do not grind crankshaft journals for extra bearing clearance, as this removes the Tufftride case. Oversized bearings are available from Chevrolet.

Table 5-2. Metal removal chart.

Cylinder Head (inches)	Intake Manifold	
	Side (inches)	Bottom (inches)
.005	.006	.009
.010	.012	.017
.015	.018	.025
.020	.025	.034
.025	.031	.043
.030	.037	.052

Chevrolet markets raw and semi-finished crankshafts in 3- and 3.5-inch stroke lengths. These forgings may be finished by competent crankshaft grinders at strokes up to 1/8-inch greater or less than their production counterparts. In addition to allowing slight increases or decreases in engine displacement, these special forgings allow the competition engine builder to obtain crankshafts with more generous fillet radii and journals of nonstandard dimensions when desired. With little or no welding on the raw forging these cranks can be ground to the proper 2.65-inch main journal diameter for use in the 4/1/8-inch bore 400 CID cylinder block.

Flywheel and Torsional Damper

Available from Chevrolet is a 15-pound nodular iron flywheel and heavy-duty 10 1/2-inch clutch. This flywheel in new condition has been tested at speeds to 10,000 rpm and is quite suitable for most small block racing applications.

You should be aware that seriously overheating a clutch significantly weakens a flywheel and rapidly lowers the burst speed at which failure could occur. Even though the Chevrolet flywheel is safe when new, it should be periodically inspected for signs of heat from the clutch and radial cracks emanating from the flywheel flange bolt holes. The lightweight flywheel may be used on the 400 CID small block *only* if the crankshaft is internally balanced or the proper unbalance weight is added to the flywheel.

Chevrolet markets two 8-inch diameter heavy-duty torsional dampers (sometimes referred to as harmonic balancers) suitable for use on high-output small block engines. In addition, a damper is marketed for the 400 CID small block with an unbalanced inertia ring to complement the stock unbalanced 400 CID crankshaft.

Many engine builders true up and/or degree mark torsional dampers, but this requires that they be rebalanced. The Chevrolet balancing specification calls for removal of material from the inertia ring with a 1/2-inch drill to a depth of 1/4 inch maximum on a radius of 3.62 inches from the hub center. Balance holes of *greater diameter or depth* may seriously weaken the damper and cause the inertia ring to fail at high engine speed.

A new 8-inch torsional damper for heavy-duty usage has been released by Chevrolet with a malleable iron inertia ring that should insure greater safety at high engine speeds. Part numbers for all dampers are shown in the Chevrolet heavy-duty parts list.

Connecting Rods

Chevrolet heavy-duty connecting rods for the small block are higher quality production parts with improved surfaces between rod and cap. In addition, they are heat treated to a greater hardness and magnaflux-inspected to be sure they are free of flaws in critical areas. All other rods should be magnafluxed before using. Rework nonfloating connecting rods for a full floating pin assembly as follows:

1. Drill 1/8-inch oil holes and counterbore the upper end 1/4-inch

2. Hone the pin hole for .0005 to .0007 inch clearance

It is a good idea to magnaflux-inspect connecting rod bolts and nuts before use, but it is a better idea to hardness test them with a Rockwell hardness tester. This is a better measure of whether or not the bolts will pull up to the proper torque. Production bolts are in the range of 36-40 Rockwell "C." Bolts not up to the minimum, or above the maximum, should not be used.

Chevrolet has a new heavy-duty connecting rod for small block racing engines. Based on the 427 rod forging, it comes correctly sized for the 2.1-inch diameter small block rod journal cranks and has no wrist pin hole machining.

The customer can have these rods finish-machined to accommodate his particular wrist pin at any rod center to the length of 5.7 to 6.150 inches. These rods have 7/16-inch diameter rod bolts and have been fatigue-tested thoroughly to prove their potential durability at high engine speeds.

To achieve minimum rod big end weight, the caps of the new rod should be lightened by machining or grinding. Typical finished cap weight should be 160 to 170 grams. Finished rod weight, after all lightening and pin hole machining, should be around 780 grams. Due to the weight of these larger rods, it is mandatory that you have your crankshaft rebalanced by an experienced engine balancer. The durability of all racing connecting rods can be improved by performing the grinding and shot peening.

As a final note, when using the new heavy-duty rod with 3.5-inch or longer strokes in the 4-inch bore block, the connecting-rod-nut-to-cylinder block clearance should be checked. If there is interference, it can be corrected by grinding the bolt head at the same angle now incorporated in the head shape. Nut clearance can be gained by installing optional 12-point aircraft nuts and/or grinding clearance in the cylinder block.

Pistons

Smooth sharp edges off the domes. For installation of rods using pressed-in wrist pins, it is preferable to heat the rod small end and install the pins quickly, using a fixture.

Most automotive machine shops and Chevrolet dealers are equipped to make this assembly. It is necessary to have at least .001-inch or preferably .0012-inch press fit between wrist pins and rods to insure that pins will not loosen and move during running. For 1969, all 302s were equipped with full floating pins, using Spirolox pin retainers, No. 3946848. Production and service wrist pins have machined flat ends for use with floating pin retainers. For competition racing, it is recommended that any racing piston be regrooved to accommodate .072-inch thick Spirolox retainers. If the grooves are machined, production or other wrist pins can be ground or turned to length to achieve the desired 0-005-inch wrist pin end float.

Note: Do not reuse wrist pin retainers after an engine has been run.

Although Chevrolet markets only 11.0 to 1 compression ratio pistons with 5/64-inch compression rings, several satisfactory designs featuring 12 to 1 and higher compression ratios with narrower ring grooves are available through reputable aftermarket piston manufacturers. You should follow the manufacturer's recommendations for piston-to-bore clearance when using these pistons.

High-compression pistons should be checked for adequate valve-to-piston clearance by assembling one piston and rod with the other engine components you plan to use (camshaft, crank, etc.). You can measure piston-to-valve clearance with small strips of clay laid across the valve notches in the piston dome while turning the engine two complete revolutions. Piston clearance of .020 inch is minimum. For drag racing and road racing it is good practice to allow more than the minimum piston-to-valve clearance to allow for occasional valve float; .100-inch is a generally accepted satisfactory minimum clearance for this usage.

Piston Rings

Chevrolet markets a high-performance low-tension ring set for the production type piston with 5/64-inch compression with 3/16-inch oil rings. These rings are high-strength iron, moly-filled with a radius contact face and are available in standard .005-, .020- and .030-inch oversizes. For narrower groove racing pistons, aftermarket high-performance parts are available.

In all cases, ring end gaps should be measured with each ring square in its cylinder bore to insure adequate end gaps to prevent ring scuffing. Minimum recommended ring end gaps are shown in the specification section. Always install compression rings with the manufacturers identification up.

The smooth bore finish currently recommended for use in all Chevrolet engines is largely a result of modern ring manufacturing techniques that virtually do away with lengthy run-in time on new engines to seat the piston rings. All rings are lapped in hardened steel cylinders during manufacture, which eliminates the need for a rough bore finish to accomplish ring seating. *Elimination of rough bores on initial build, and rehoning on rebuild, results in a sizeable power increase* due to decreased engine friction. See the bore finishing specifications.

Valve Lifters

For high-performance hydraulic camshafts, use production Chevrolet lifters and lash 1/2 to 3/4 turn after rocker arm slack is taken up. If all new parts are used, hydraulic lifters should be relashed after 1000-2000 miles to compensate for run-in wear. Added engine limiting speed can be attained with hydraulic lifter cams by zero lashing the lifters. This requires idling a warmed-up engine and backing off the lash adjusting nut until the clicking just disappears, and then to 1/8 turn tighter. Repeat this operation for each valve.

Two Chevrolet production mechanical valve lifters are available. Lifter No. 5232695 has a similar external appearance to a hydraulic valve lifter and overhead oil metering is controlled by an internal inertia flapper valve (piddle valve). This is production in most Z-28 302 cubic inch engines. Also available is lifter No. 5231585 used in 1959-65 high-performance 327 cubic inch engines and late 302 engines. This lifter meters overhead oil on the basis of lifter-to-bore clearance orificing, and has several desirable features not available with the piddle valve lifter.

Lifter No. 5231585 effects a 10-20% reduction in *total* oil circulation rate due to its design, and is recommended for use with needle roller rocker arms. This can be a considerable benefit in dry sump and restricted oil pan capacity installations. If conventional rocker arms are used, lifter No. 5231585 may still be used to advantage by grinding or turning a 1/16 × .030-inch deep groove around the lifter connecting the oil feed holes approximately 1/8 inch above the wide groove already in the lifter body. This will increase overhead lubrication enough for production rocker arms.

It is recommended that Molykote or other molydisulfide based EP lubricant be used on lifters for proper break-in. In addition, valve lifters will be more compatible with the camshaft if you polish the contact surface with No. 600 grit sandpaper before installing them. Good used lifters that still retain some crown or convex curvature across the bottom are very satisfactory.

Camshaft

Chevrolet offers several camshafts applicable to street high-performance and racing uses. The chart below indicates the specifications and general usage of all high-performance camshafts.

Production nylon camshaft sprocket and chain are used by many engine builders. A wider chain and cast iron cam sprocket may be obtained by ordering replacement items for pre-1967 model V-8 engines. High quality roller chain kits are also available from aftermarket parts dealers.

If you intend to adjust the timing of your camshaft from the production timing locators, kits are available from aftermarket high-performance parts dealers that use offset crankshaft keys, or offset camshaft locator dowels. Instructions for their use may not be included, and you should have proper degree wheels and dial indicators available to check your camshaft timing before and after changing it. You should also be aware that as you advance cam timing relative to the crankshaft, the intake valve-to-piston clearance is reduced; and as you retard camshaft timing, the exhaust valve-to-piston clearance is reduced.

Molykote or other molydisulfied-based grease should be used to coat the cam lobes during assembly. With very high-performance camshafts, the initial run-in is very critical and the engine should not be allowed to idle below 2000 rpm for the first half hour of running time. If, after following our recommendations for cam and lifter preparation, you have trouble with early cam lobe failure, you may have to run-in the cam and lifters with reduced valve spring loads, and change to racing valve springs after an hour or so of run-in.

Valve Springs and Retainers

Chevrolet markets only a production V-8 valve spring and damper, and a dual-coil high-performance spring listed in the Chevrolet heavy-duty parts section. The production spring is preferred for all hydraulic and street use mechanical lifter cams. Measure spring space and shim for correct installed height of 1.720 inch. Production specifications for spring loads is 76-84 to 1.70 lb./in and 194-206 to 1.25 lb./in. spring space. Use a production steel cap and umbrella shield for oil control.

Recent service high-performance cylinder heads have been machined to accept Chevrolet's dual-coil valve spring which uses an aluminum alloy valve spring cap. This spring supplies greater loads for racing camshafts and should be installed at 1.720 inches. Average blueprint specification loads on this spring are 135 pounds and 290 pounds at 0.5-inch lift. These springs will extend the rev range of the two Chevrolet racing camshafts to 8000 rpm.

Aftermarket flat tappet and roller tappet camshafts may require different valve springs and their manufacturer's recommendations should be followed in the absence of proof that Chevrolet springs are satisfactory.

Valve Train

Production high-performance push rods have a hardened steel inserted tip in one end, and should be installed with this end up. The Chevrolet rocker arm is not serviced separately, but is part of a unit consisting of one rocker arm, ball and adjusting nut. The Chevrolet rocker arm has a raised letter "V" forged inside the pallet end.

Production rocker arm adjusting nuts are preferred over any other type for production rockers; however, they must have sufficient preload torque so that they won't back off while the engine is running. Any nuts with low preload should be discarded.

Nineteen seventy and later die cast aluminum rocker arm covers have cast-in drippers to improve rocker arm ball lubrication. New valve train parts experience considerable valve lash during run-in, and lash should be checked and corrected frequently until it stabilizes. New rocker arms and balls should be observed closely for overheating and excessive wear during run-in.

If necessary to change a rocker and ball, always install a good used run-in rocker and ball. If no good used ones are available, move an intake rocker and ball over to the burned exhaust position and install the new parts on an intake position which runs cooler. Always keep good run-in rocker arms and balls together during engine disassembly and rebuild. Several aftermarket parts dealers carry grooved rocker balls which may show better resistance to overheating with high valve spring loads.

Most current designs of needle roller rocker arms are recommended for all-out racing. They offer some reduction in engine oil temperature, and allow a reduction in overhead oil required for adequate lubrication. For high valve spring load installation, 7/16-inch rocker arm studs, as used on the Chevrolet 396-454 CID engines, are recommended with needle roller rocker arms.

Cylinder Head Gasket

Chevrolet offers three cylinder head gasket designs for 4-inch bore engines and two designs for 4 1/8-inch bore engines.

1. The production gasket of steel shim design with raised beads around bores and water passages. Recommended for stock and mildly modified engines; approximately .018-inch thick.

2. A stainless steel shim design similar to production types, except for material; recommended for many high-performance and racing engines and marine use where maximum power is not used for long periods. For 4-inch bore engines only, approximately .107-inch thick.

3. A stainless steel and asbestos composition gasket of sandwich type construction (two layers of stainless with composition material between). Suitable for all racing and marine use on 4- and 4 1/8-inch bore engines; approximately .039-inch compressed thickness.

4. The production 4 1/8-inch bore gasket of stainless steel and red or black composition material featuring steel beads around the bores only. Recommended for stock or mildly modified 4 1/8-inch bore blocks only; .039-inch compressed thickness.

All head gaskets should be installed with a commercial head gasket sealer. High-compression engines may benefit by using aluminum paint for a gasket sealer. Steel shim gaskets do not need retorquing, but all sandwich and composition gaskets should be retorqued (either hot or cold) after the first warm up.

Engine Lubrication

When properly assembled and installed in a vehicle with the correct oil pan, pump, coolers and filters, the Chevrolet small block is remarkably free of any failures from the lubrication system.

The *basic* requirement to guarantee freedom from excessive bearing wear and failures is a steady *non-fluctuating* supply of clean oil between 150 and 270° F temperature at 65-80 psi. All modifications to the engine oiling system in a race car, boat, or other high-performance applications are done to achieve the above basic requirements.

The desired 65-80 psi oil pressure is governed by the oil pump bypass relief valve. Clean oil is insured by filtering the oil before it goes to the engine with a non-bypassing filter, either engine or remote mounted. The proper oil temperature is controlled by engine warmup before racing, and the use of an oil cooler, if required, to keep the oil temperature below 270°.

The final most difficult basic requirement is a steady oil pressure supply. The majority of engine bearing failures are a direct result of oil pressure loss due to the oil pump picking up air while the car is negotiating turns at racing speeds. This occurs at a time when the driver is busiest and may go unreported, or be reported as a slight drop in oil pressure in the turns. Good gauge response is necessary to troubleshoot this problem and the gauge should be mounted as close to the driver's line of vision as is practical. The oil pressure gauge line should be a minimum of 1/8-inch ID to get good gauge response and help detect any oil pressure losses quickly.

Oil pressure loss in turns is aggravated by three things:

1. Insufficient oil level or capacity.

2. High engine oil flow rates due to excessive bearing clearances, or higher than necessary oil pressure.

3. Improper oil pan baffling, usually over-baffling which prevents the engine oil from properly draining back into the oil pan while the car is in a turn.

Oil Pump

On the lower end of the pickup tube, some sort of a flat, round pickup shield similar to production types should be used to keep it from picking up air along with the oil. The pickup may be repositioned for the specific use the engine will see. For oval track operation it may be located on the right side of the pan and for drag racing to the rear of the pan. The pickup tube should be welded into the body of the pump. The production high-performance oil pressure bypass spring will usually supply enough oil pressure even with a remote oil filter and cooler. Any oil pressure greater than 65 psi at operating speed is sufficient for high-performance use. In any case, oil pressure should not be greater than 80 psi.

You may shim the oil pressure bypass spring to increase pressure by installing small washers inside the bypass piston. Be careful not to use so many spacers that the bypass piston will not uncover the bypass port in the oil pump cover. To do so will result in very high cold oil pressure, which may blow out the oil filter seal or cause excessive distributor gear wear due to high loading.

Oil Pan

Modify the oil pan as desired for increased capacity. Run a semicircular piece of flat Corvette tray baffle and some form of baffle attached to the lower step of the oil pan to retard oil sloshing on brake stops. Production Z28 302 engine oil pans have excellent baffling already built in, and have proven satisfactory in competition use. If available, a magnetic drain plug whould be installed. Overfilling the oil pan to gain capacity is not recommended. It may cause oil to overheat rapidly, and oil pressure fluctuation will occur in straightaway acceleration.

Oil Cooler

If desired, an oil cooler can be plumbed into the engine, using a cooler available from Chevrolet parts and accessories. Adapters to use in place of the production oil filter or remote oil filters to take off, filter, cool, and return oil to the engine are available through high-performance and marine parts manufacturers. In all installations, at least 1/2-inch ID line should be used and the oil filtered just before it is returned to the engine to prevent contamination of the engine bearings. Any in-and-out and remote filter adapters should be designed or reworked to eliminate any pressure bypass valves, thereby preventing any circulating oil from bypassing the oil filter. They should also be accurately checked to insure that

Fig. 5-3. With enough power to literally lift the front wheels off the ground, Z28 is a good choice for competition.

they completely seal in the upper cavity of the oil filter pad on the cylinder block to eliminate partial bypassing.

A satisfactory oil cooler adapter is marketed by Chevrolet which can be installed between the cylinder block and oil filter to provide taps for connecting the oil cooler lines.

Dry Sump Oiling System

Some types of racing require the use of a dry sump oiling system (USAC sprint and championship cars, for example). And some types of racing, such as road racing with minimal oil pan space, demand the use of a dry sump system to meet the basic requirement for steady oil pressure supply. The following tips should be of assistance with any commercially available dry sump unit you may use:

1. If possible, eliminate the engine oil pump completely and install a non-bypassing in-and-out adapter to the oil filter pad at the rear of the engine.

2. Most dry sump oil pumps are a combination of pressure and two or three scavenger pump stages contained in a single belt-driven unit. The small block pump should have at least two and preferably three scavenger section plus the pressure section.

3. Two scavenger stages should scavenge the oil pan. If available a third stage can connect to the rear outside of the rocker

cover on the predominant outboard side of the car. (This depends on the course and whether it is run clockwise or counterclockwise).

4. With adequate scavenge capacity you can pass scavenged oil through the oil cooler on its return to the supply tank. To do this, however, you must have low restriction oil coolers. Do not connect oil coolers in series. If more than one oil cooler is used, they should be connected in parallel (i.e., tee the oil line and pass the oil into and out of both coolers simultaneously.) Use at least a No. 12 or 3/4-inch ID scavenge line from the pump to the supply tank. You may wish to install a screen-type aircraft filter in this line to keep from getting contaminants into the supply tank, pressure pump, and pressure bypass valve.

5. Use a No. 12 or 3/4-inch inlet line to the pressure pump from the supply tank.

6. Direct the oil from the pressure pump through the remote filter and into the engine. It is permissible and satisfactory to install the oil cooler between the pressure pump and the remote oil filter. Use No. 10 or 1/2-inch ID oil lines for high-pressure oil routing.

7. Do not try to run more than 65-70 psi oil pressure while hot. This will aggravate oil aeration and impair the oil scavenging. Oil pressure over 65 psi is not necessary for good bearing life.

8. Ran a full length semicircular trap baffle under the crankshaft with louvers to draw the oil away from the crank, if no similar baffle is counted in the oil pan.

9. A round oil sump tank design is preferred, made as small in diameter and tall as space permits with a capacity of at least eight quarts when two thirds full. It should have a cone-shaped bottom with the oil outlet to the pressure pump in the bottom of the tank. This design will assure that the oil outlet is covered under all "G" loads the vehicle will be subjected to. The scavenged oil should be returned to the supply tank near the top of the tank tangent to the side of the tank, as indicated by the arrow. This will cause the oil to circulate around the side of the tank, aiding in separating the air from the scavenged oil. The tank should also incorporate a horizontal baffle with 3/16- to 1/4-inch holes through its surface to help de-aerate the oil and stop the swirling of the returned oil.

10. Build the engine with the proper lifters, rocker arms, and clearances to require a minimum of oil flow. This is the greatest asset to a properly functioning dry sump system.

Fig. 5-4. Blueprinting is a must for the preparation of any engine for competition. Blueprinting means making sure the tolerances are perfect in all components and that all clearances are set to optimum for competition.

11. Vent both the engine and the supply tank, or vent the engine to a properly vented supply tank. Keep vent lines of adequate size (1 No. 12 or 1 No. 10 size lines) to prevent any pressure buildup in the crankcase. *This is a common mistake.* Existing breather holes in the engine rocker covers are an excellent place to vent from. Leave the production oil separators in the rocker covers under the vent holes.

12. If at all possible, run the complete dry sump on a dynamometer with a simple sight tube gauge on the side of the sump tank to determine any oil level fluctuation. This will confirm the design of your oil pan and baffles for satisfactory scavenging. There should be no more than 2-3 quarts drop between idle and maximum engine speed. You can make a similar test by shutting off and declutching the engine at high speed in a vehicle, and draining the oil pan to determine how much oil remains in the engine.

The fact that you have a dry sump on the engine does not guarantee trouble-free operation. You must be sure the dry sump system is operating properly, and this includes use of the oil pressure gauge to observe pressure flunctuations and tests to insure good scavenging.

Intake Manifold

The most efficient intake manifold sold by Chevrolet was used on the 1967-71 Z/28 Camaro 302 and 350 CID engines. This manifold is an aluminum high rise, tuned runner type, designed to mount a single Holley 4-barrel carburetor. Any size Holley from 500-960 CFM airflow can be mounted. Stock carburetor is a 780 CFM Model 4053 or 3943. No manifold porting is necessary, but opening of ports to match manifold gasket and head ports is recommended. Do not remove the center divider from the manifold below the carburetor to a depth greater than one inch.

Carburetor

Use the special 830 CFM Holley listed in the parts section. This carburetor has 1 11/16-inch throttle bores, mechanically operated secondaries, and accelerator pumps on both primary and secondary barrels. Satisfactory jetting for most running conditions is achieved with No. 77 jets in both the primary and secondaries. If a richer or leaner mixture is desired, change all jets up or down in size. Also available are aftermarket Holley racing carburetors with mechanically operated secondary throttles and double accelerator pumps. Similar jetting should be suitable for these carburetors as well.

The production sintered bronze fuel filters located inside the fuel inlet nuts at each end of Holley carburetors should be removed and discarded. In their place install a single large paper-element replaceable filter between the fuel pump and carburetor. The fuel pressure drop through the production bronze filters as they become plugged cannot be detected since the filters are located after the pressure gauge connection. *This one item* has accounted for a large number of engine failures and poor performance in the past. Fuel lines should be neoprene rubber, aeroquip, or steel. *Never* use copper tubing as it will eventually crack. A fuel pressure gauge should be installed between the fuel filter and carburetor, and fuel pressure of at least 4 psi maintained at maximum speed, wide-open throttle.

In operating conditions where fresh air is ducted to the carburetor (fresh air hoods, plenum air cleaners, etc.), it is necessary that a foam or paper low-restriction air cleaner element be used to diffuse the air entering the carburetor. If no diffuser is used, the engine mixture distribution will be upset, causing poor power and misfiring at high engine speeds.

Fuel Pump

If possible, use an electric fuel pump to boost (or in place of) the engine mechanical fuel pump. The 1963-65 Corvette high-performance fuel pump shown in the Chevrolet parts list is the most satisfactory for high-performance usage. Adequate capacity electric fuel pumps are not available from aftermarket high-performance parts manufacturers.

Distributor

All Chevrolet engines prior to 1975 were equipped with conventional breaker point type distributors. In 1969, the basic distributors were converted to aluminum housings, except for Corvette, which retained a cast iron mechanical tach drive distributor until 1975.

If you intend to use a mechanical tachometer, any pre-1975 Corvette distributor can be used, including the dual-breaker point design shown in the heavy duty parts section. For racing, the transistorized ignition with magnetic pulse distributor offered as an option by Chevrolet since 1965 is preferred. Several tach drive versions are shown in the Chevrolet heavy duty parts list, along with the transistor ignition unit required to complete the system. In addition, any breaker point distributor can be converted to magnetic pulse by using the stationary and rotating pole pieces shown in the Chevrolet parts list.

The 1975 high-energy ignition is a transistorized ignition with special heavy-duty temperature-resistant plug wires and boots. It should be an excellent racing unit. However, it does not have a mechanical tach drive, and its physical size may interfere with your air cleaner where only limited under-hood space is available. For best all around operation, you should tailor your distributor advance curve. Do not connect the vacuum advance unit.

An excellent spark plug wire kit with high-temperature silicone wires and boots and stainless steel wire is available from Chevrolet with either straight or 90° angle boots. All wires are long and may be cut to length by the customer.

The transistorized ignition trouble diagnosis procedure will aid in defining any trouble you may encounter with the pre-1975 breakerless ignition.

High Energy Ignition System

The main features of the high energy ignition system (HEI) are described below. During servicing, the cover and cap need not be separated except to replace one of these components or to replace the coil.

A magnetic pickup assembly located over the shaft contains a permanent magnet, a pole piece with internal teeth, and a pickup coil. When the teeth of the timer core rotating inside the pole piece line up and separate with the teeth of the pole piece, an induced voltage in the pickup coil signals the all-electronic module to open the ignition coil primary circuit. The primary current decreases and a high voltage is induced in the ignition coil secondary winding, which is directed through the rotor and high-voltage leads to fire the spark plugs. The capacitor suppresses radio noise.

The magnetic pickup assembly is mounted over the main bearing on the distributor housing, and is made to rotate by the vacuum control unit, thus providing vacuum advance. The timer core is made to rotate about the shaft by conventional advance weights, thus providing centrifugal advance.

Important: When making compression checks, disconnect the ignition switch connector from HEI System.

No periodic lubrication is required. Engine oil lubricates the lower bushing and an oil-filled reservoir provides lubrication for the upper bushing.

Exhaust System

A well designed and constructed open exhaust system, with similar length primary pipes of the correct length and diameter, is mandatory for a racing engine. Correct dimensions for such a system are 1 3/4-inch OD by 30-inch long head pipes collected in a group into 3 1/4-inch to 3 1/2-inch collector tailpipe. Three-and-one-half-inch tailpipe is preferred for any installation requiring more than 36 inches of tailpipe. Several header systems designed to these dimensions are currently being marketed by speed shops and high-performance parts manufacturers. Fuel-injected or Weber-carbureted engines respond favorably to 1 7/8-inch OD head pipes 32-34 inches long with 3 1/2- to 4-inch tailpies.

In limited-space installations, where less than 3 1/2-inch tailpipes can be used, a crossover pipe of 2 1/2- to 3-inches diameter between tailpipes just behind the collectors will measurably increase power.

Engine Run-In

Racing engines should be run-in for at least an hour and preferably two hours. Any type of running between 2000 and 4000 rpm will be of benefit, but a dynamometer controlled run-in is best of all. This allows a controlled load on the engine, and any oil and water leaks or other deficiencies in build-up are more easily repaired. Thirty weight oil and street-type heat range spark plugs should be used during run-in.

After run-in, spark plugs, oil and filter should be changed and the valve train inspected and valves relashed. If a head gasket retorque is required, it can be done at this time before the valves are relashed. Inspect the drain oil and filter for large foreign particles at this time also.

It is particularly important that you change the oil filter, because if you followed our recommendation on build-up lubricants and plugging the oil filter bypass, the filter will be plugged with Molykote during run-in. This will show up as a decrease in engine oil pressure.

An engine that has just been rebuilt with new piston rings and a used camshaft needs little or no run-in, a warm-up and hot lash is sufficient.

Table 5-3 lists recommended bolt torque and lubricant specifications.

Operating Conditions

Following are several recommended operating specifications and limits that should insure long and satisfactory service from an engine built as described by these instructions.

Oil—30 to 50 weight aircraft or other ashless high-performance oil (Valvoline, etc.). An oil with ashless additives is specified to prevent preignition and burnt pistons.

Fuel—The best super premium available. Examples are 260 Sunoco, 100-130 octane aviation gas, or Union 76 racing gasoline.

Fig. 5-5. Some engine modifications are fine for certain kinds of competition. But don't try to run this carburetion setup on the street.

Aviation fuel and racing gasoline have carefully controlled vapor pressure to prevent vapor lock. Some pump fuels, particularly in northern climates, will cause vapor lock and lean mixtures if you happen to get fuel tailored for cold weather use.

Spark plugs—track racing, A.C. 436TS or 438TS; drag racing, AC 441TS or 443TS or R42T.

Spark advance—Maximum of 36 to 40°.

Valve lash—As specified in the text for each camshaft.

Maximum speed with racing cams—68-7600 for track racing, 8000 for drag racing.

Maximum oil temperature—300° in the oil pan.

Minimum fuel pressure—4-5 psi at high engine speeds.

Recommended Clearances

Piston to bore (Chevrolet forged pistons): .005-.0055 inch measured at the wrist-pin centerline hole, perpendicular to the pin. Finish bores with No. 500 grit stones or equivalent (smooth).

Piston ring: Minimum and clearance—top, .022; second, .016; oil, .016.

Wrist pin: .0004-.0008 inch in piston; .0005-.0007 inch in rod for floating pin; 0-.005-inch end play preferred.

Rod bearing: .002-.0025 inch; side clearance, .010-.020.

Table 5-3. Recommended bolt torque and lubricant specifications for small block V-8s with head No. 3965784.

	Torque	Lubricant
Main bearing	inner 70 .lb./ft.	Molykote
	outer 65	Molykote
Connecting rod bolt (⅜-inch)	45-50 lb./ft. (.006-inch stretch preferred)	oil
Connecting rod bolt (7/16-inch)	60-65 lb./ft.	oil
Cylinder head bolt	65 lb./ft.	sealant
Rocker arm stud (late HP head)	50 lb./ft.	sealant
Camshaft sprocket	20 lb./ft.	oil
Intake manifold	30 lb./ft.	oil
Flywheel	60 lb./ft.	oil
Spark plugs (conventional gasket)	25 lb./ft.	dry
Spark plugs (tapered seat)	15 lb./ft.	dry
Exhaust Manifold	25 lb./ft.	Antisieze
Oil pan bolt	165 lb./in.	oil
Front cover bolt	75 lb./in.	oil
Rocker cover	25 lb./in.	oil

Main bearing: .002-.003 inch, minimum preferred; .005-.007-inch end play.

Piston to top of block (deck height): .015-.020 inch average below deck. No part of the piston except the dome is to be higher than the deck of the block. Deck height specified is for a .018-inch steel head gasket; if a thicker head gasket is used, piston-to-bylinder head clearance of .035 inch should be considered minimum.

Valve lash: As shown in the text for each camshaft.

Valve to piston clearance: .020-inch exhaust and intake at zero valve lash. *Note:* These are to be considered absolute minimum clearances for an engine to run below the valve train limiting speed of 8000 rpm. If you intend to run up to the valve train limiting speed, more clearance should be allowed. It is common practice to allow .100-inch intake exhaust valve clearance for engines used in drag racing.

Chapter 6
Chassis Preparation
For Racing

The following preparations and modifications will make a Z28 ready for racing.

For the 1970-80 Camaro, a full-size passenger car axle with 8 ⅞-inch ring gear should be used. The unit can be modified for disc brakes and to utlize the 1969 springs.

REAR AXLE

Axle assemblies without parking brake provisions must not be installed in vehicles that will be driven on public highways or streets. Laws in many states will hold the vehicle operator responsible for operating his vehicle without parking brakes in addition to the regular service brakes.

REAR SPRINGS

The 1967-69 average load/rate for base rear springs is 125 in./lb.

SUBFRAME PREPARATION—CAMARO 1970-80

The front subframe should be removed from the car for preparation. Thoroughly clean (sand-blast preferably) the subframe and weld all seams not completely welded. If regulations permit, reinforcement of the spring seat and the upper control arm mounting bracket should be done. Check the shock absorber clearance hole in the upper spring seat to insure adequate clearance around the shock absorbers.

Eliminate the rubber body mounts and make aluminum or steel spacers to space the subframe in its normal position relative to the unit body. Some regulations prohibit bolting or welding the

Fig. 6-1. The Z28 Camaro is stable at any speed for normal driving.

subframe solidly against the body. It is very important to use the metal spacers to eliminate flexing between the subframe and body for improved handling and safety.

The 1970 subframe is modified to accept heavy-duty coil springs and to provide control arm clearance.

FRONT SUSPENSION—CAMARO 1970-80

Each organization allows different changes in the front suspension mounting points or other dimensions. Check with individual organizations for specific rulings in this area.

It is recommended that all rubber control are bushings be replaced with bronze, aluminum or high-density plastic bushings to

Fig. 6-2. The car in stock condition corners flat and generates high cornering power. However, for all out competition, chassis modifications are necessary.

Fig. 6-3. Note the flat cornering attitude of this '74.

eliminate suspension compliance under cornering loads. This will allow you to achieve better tire contact from both front wheels while cornering. Care must be taken in the design of such bushings to prevent clearance from developing through wear. High-quality ball joints and tie-rod ends are listed in the Chevrolet HD parts list,

Fig. 6-4. For all out competition, there is still too much understeer built into the chassis. Modifications can make the chassis race ready.

Fig. 6-5. Here, the author pushes the Z through a tight turn during a test session. Note understeering attitude.

as well as Tufftride heat-treated knuckles (pre-1970) which have proven their durability. For 1970 Camaros, service knuckles are available which allow use of Corvette disc and caliper.

Fig. 6-6. The modifications described in this chapter are for those readers who want to know how to set up a chassis for racing. On the street and over the road, the Z28 is a fine handling, stable machine.

143

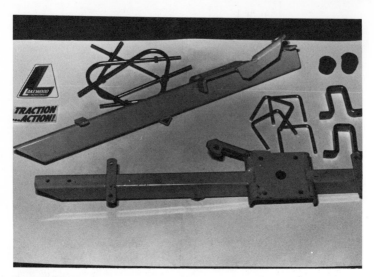

Fig. 6-7. One modification that is useful even for the street is a set of rear traction bars to prevent rear spring windup on hard acceleration.

Some method should be used to retain the lower ball joint in addition to the press fit in the lower control arm. A retaining strap

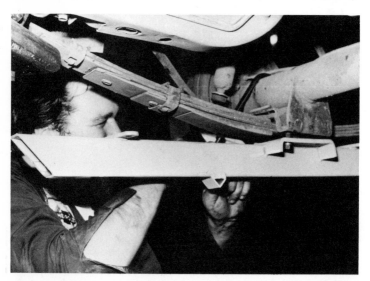

Fig. 6-8. Bars bolt to the leaf spring to prevent the spring from "wrapping around" the axle and hopping under hard acceleration. Later models, 1977-up, are not bothered by this problem because of the lower power of the smog-free engines.

across the bottom or tack welding have been used successfully. Front-wheel alignment settings are listed in a separate section. Optional size antisway bars are available up to 1 1/16-inch OD (pre-1970). Satisfactory handling has been achieved with these bars in production rubber mounting bushings and with production rubber cushioned links. For pre-1970 cars, no heavy-duty antisway bars are available. The front ride height should be roughly 9 1/2 inches from ground to inner forward A-arm bolt (pre-1970). For 1970 and up, minimum ground clearance to subframe cross member should be 3 1/2 inches. Care should be taken to assure enough bump travel at this height.

FRONT SPRINGS

The 1967-1969 average load/rate for base front springs is 347 pounds. Comparison can be made with the following special springs.

The 1970-80 off-the-road front springs should be fabricated by using .75-inch diameter wire. Coil the spring to a 5.58 inches O.D. and 7.67 coils at a free height of 12.17 inches; fabricated in this fashion, the load/rate will be 650 in./lb., This spring should be used with related components as noted and referenced to the knuckles.

An optional spring already fabricated can be obtained from independent sources. This optional spring has a load/rate of 600 in./lb., 5.50-inches diameter, eight coils and a free height of 12.50 inches. Adjust the bump rubber height to limit spring travel so the tie rod does not contact frame.

REAR SUSPENSION

Several rear spring rates are available from the Chevrolet heavy-duty parts list. Pre-1970 optional rear springs can be used in 1970 cars. Forward and rear spring eye bushings should be of monoballs, aluminum or delrin rather than rubber, to help properly position the rear axle and reduce axle tramp under braking.

The rear axle should be attached to the springs with U-bolts available in the Chevrolet heavy-duty parts list. Rear body height may be adjusted with lowering blocks or by having the spring re-arched in a spring shop. Lowering blocks can be eliminated and an improvement in rear axle tramp under braking can be achieved by having the front spring eyes re-rolled so that center line of the eye is on the center line of the main leaf. This also can be done by most spring shops. In any event, allow at least three inches of bump travel, measured from the top of the axle to the bottom of the underbody where the axle will hit under severe jounce.

There are no heavy-duty rear anti-roll bars offered as service parts. Panhard rods, Watt linkages, and traction bars or radius rods are allowed by most organizations. The need for these items must be determined by the chassis builder and is subject to driver preference.

The preceding refers to the heavy-duty rear axle for pre-1970 cars. For '70 up there is no optional disc brake rear axle. But you can convert to a full-size Chevrolet rear axle (8 7/8-inch ring gear) and use Corvette 4-wheel discs and calipers. This conversion will result in a rear tread width of 64.00 inches with zero offset wheels. Shot peening of axles and frequent magnifluxing is necessary.

Quick-change axles are allowed and floater hubs are required by various organizations.

Rear axle temperatures should be monitored and a cooler with auxiliary pump should be incorporated if the temperature exceeds 325°F.

For satisfactory gear life, 50 to 100 miles of light load break-in running is mandatory. D. A. Speed Sport 90W gear lube has been used with satisfactory results.

SPRING AND SWAY BAR RATES

Spring rates as follows work well and are a good starting combination:

Front: 500-600 lb./in. with a 7/8-inch, 15/16-inch or 1-inch sway bar

Rear: 200-250 lb./in.

For high "G" loads, the following combination should be satisfactory:

Front: 725 lb./in. with a 7/8-inch sway bar

Rear: 300 lb./in.

As a general rule of thumb, if the front end pushes or understeers excessively, the front roll rate should be decreased by the use of softer springs or a small sway bar; or the rear roll rate can be increased by the installation of stiffer rear springs or sway bar (if one is used). Conversely, if the car oversteers or tends to spin out too readily, the installation of softer rear springs or higher rate front springs or sway bar is called for. Some degree of understeer control can be achieved by camber changes. More negative camber reduces understeer.

The general consensus is that a slightly understeering car that requires some application of power to achieve oversteer is the most satisfactory balance for good handling and maximum speed.

When selecting spring rates, keep in mind that under no anticipated cornering loads should the suspension or shock absorbers bottom out. This will cause immediate oversteer or understeer, depending on whether the rear or front bottoms, and a wild ride—if not complete loss of control. Trimming or removal of bump stops will increase suspension travel over production limits and may be accompanied by bump stops on the shock absorbers.

WHEELS

For pre-1970, the offset to retain maximum rear tread width with minimum fender rework is .20-.25-inch positive. For the front wheels, a negative .20-.25 offset will give improved wheel bearing life, easier steering, and minimum fender rework.

One-half inch × 20 × 1 3/4 inch wheel stud bolts are available for improved durability under part No. 3849110 for front wheels and may also be used for rear hubs if the splines are shortened to .40-inch length. (The rear brake disc should not ride on the splined section of the wheel stud bolts.)

Alternate wheel stud bolts are available under part No. 3819780. These are 2 7/8 inches long, 1/2-inch × 20 bolts. It is necessary to shorten the spline on these bolts as required to fit the hubs. Use of these bolts and special lug nuts (available from wheel manufacturers) will facilitate quick wheel changes with power wrenches.

FRONT END GEOMETRY AND CHASSIS BALANCE

Recommended front wheel geometry settings are:
Camber: 2-3 1/2° negative, all models
Caster: 3-5° positive, pre-1970, 2-3 ° positive, 1970
Toe: 1/16-1/8 toe-out, all models
The chassis should be adjusted to provide approximately equal weight on both rear wheels with the driver seated in the car. This can be accomplished with various length rear spring shackles or by shimming or trimming the front springs. This measurement and adjustment should be accomplished with the anti-roll bars unhooked. Anti-roll bars should be reconnected in such a manner that they do not preload the chassis.

Chapter 7

The Ultra Z

Call them what you will. Show cars. Experimentals models. Prototypes. One-offs. The fact remains that Chevrolet loves to build them, and car enthusiasts everywhere love to look at—and hopefully buy—them. Chevrolet's been building them since 1953 (the first Corvette) and we've been loving it ever since.

The latest in a long line of special Chevrolets is of more than passing interest to Camaro Z28 lovers. In fact, it's perhaps the most significant Chevrolet experimental vehicle ever built, if you love Z28s. It's almost certain that many of the design ideas in this experimental one-off Z-car will be incorporated into future Z28 models from Chevrolet.

Chevy sprung it on the press during their long-lead new model preview in the summer of 1979. They called it the Ultra Z. It is, in many respects, the ultimate Z28 Camaro. It's certainly the most sophisticated from an engineering point of view, with all kinds of little tidbits to make your mouth drool.

Happily for the author, he was at the 1979 Chevrolet press preview of new models and was not only able to photograph the ultimate Z but also drive it.

As you can see from the photos (Figs. 7-1 through 7-10), the Ultra Z is not radically different from an exterior view, although there are some interesting design ideas we'll describe in a bit. What is exciting is what's under the hood (Figs. 7-11 and 7-12).

Chevrolet engineering pulled out all the stops on this one and not only built a screamer of a show car, but also incorporated all the

Fig. 7-1. The Ultra Z at highway speed.

key buzz word features and design cues that car enthusiasts love so much. As such, the Ultra Z is the world's only aluminum-engined, fuel-injected, turbo supercharged Z28. Sound interesting? You bet!

THE ENGINE

The engine looks like a standard 350 cubic inch (5.7 liter) small block Z28 engine. In most specs, it is. The bore and stroke are stock at 4.00-inch and 3.48-inch. Compression ratio is a sedate 8.4 to 1. Now here's where things get interesting.

The cylinder block is not made of standard, run-of-the-mill cast iron. Instead, it's cast of aluminum with cast iron liners. This cylinder block is supposedly available on a limited basis from Chevrolet Parts to anyone who wants one. The cylinder heads are standard angle-plug high-performance heads with screw-in studs and 2.02-inch intake valves and 1.60-inch exhaust valves and big

Fig. 7-2. The author after a test session with the Ultra Z at GM's Milford Michigan Proving Ground facility.

Fig. 7-3. The Ultra Z has features that will probably be incorporated into future production Z28s.

ports. However, the cylinder heads, too, are cast in aluminum. These are not available. At least, not as of this writing.

Fig. 7-4. The louvered hood and "turbo" insignia are plainly visible here.

Fig. 7-5. The front end is relatively stock. The wheels are experimental 8-inch versions of stock production wheels.

The engine also has experimental pistons made by TRW especially cast to be used in turbocharged engines. The bottom end of the engine consists of a stock L-82 forged crankshaft with 4-bolt mains and L-82 connecting rods.

To prevent damage via severe detonation due to the relatively high compression ratio and turbocharger setup, a prototype detonation sensor is tied into the stock high energy ignition system. When the sensor determines that detonation is setting in, it

Fig. 7-6. The tires are 60-series steel-belted radials.

automatically cuts back on the spark advance by 2-degree intervals until the detonation ceases. Thus, the engine runs at optimum spark advance at all times.

The turbocharger itself is an AiResearch model T-3. The T-3 incorporates an integral waste gate which bleeds off pressure if the

Fig. 7-7. The lean, sleek look of the Ultra Z is pictured here. Louvers really work.

Fig. 7-8. From the back, the Ultra Z tells the world that this is a turbo Camaro.

manifold pressure reaches higher than 7 psi of boost. The turbocharger is mounted directly to the right-hand cast iron exhaust manifold which was modified to take the turbo mounting.

The intake system is a specially calibrated Bendix (Cadillac) timed electonic fuel injection system with closed-loop electronic air/fuel ratio control. Fuel is injected directly into each intake port. The air throttle valve is located at the turbocharger compress inlet.

The closed-loop system consists of sensors at various critical engine locations and also in the tailpipe. The sensors monitor such things as spark advance, fuel pressure, HC, CO and NOx volumes, manifold pressure, etc. Then the sensors send the information to the on-board computer which then tells the fuel injection unit precisely how much fuel to inject at any given moment. Not only does this make engine combustion much more fuel efficient, it also controls emissions more efficiently.

The exhaust gases dump into a stock 1979 exhaust system minus the stock catalytic converter. The Z28's stock system is very efficient in that it uses 2½-inch pipe all the way back to the rear bumper with only twin resonators to create any back pressure.

TRANSMISSION

The Ultra Z's transmission is a stock Turbo Hydra-Matic 350. The rest of the drivetrain is also stock, with a production 3.42 rear axle ratio with limited-slip differential.

CHASSIS

The chassis is mostly stock, too, with springs, shocks and stabilizer bars straight from a stock 1979 Z28. The biggest change is in the wheel and tire department. Stock Z-cars have P225/70R15 steel-belted radials on 15 × 7 wheels. The Ultra Z has superwide P255/60R15 Goodyear Eagle GTs mounted on 15 × 8 wheels of the stock design but made of aluminum.

Fig. 7-9. The whale tail rear deck spoiler is experimental, but will probably appear on future production Z-cars.

Fig. 7-10. The 350 cubic inch LM-1 engine is fuel injected and turbocharged.

BODY

The Ultra Z's body sports special metallic blue paint with graphics (Figs. 7-13 to 7-16) by the Chevrolet design staff. You'll also spot a prototype rear deck lid spoiler and a stock Z28 front air

Fig. 7-11. The fuel injection system is a Bendix unit off a Cadillac Seville. Estimated output is 300 real horesepower.

dam. Inside, the steering wheel is an experimental design and covered with leather. The Ultra Z weighs 3599 pounds, while you'll find a stock street-ready Z28 Camaro weighing in around 3800 pounds. The aluminum works.

DRIVING THE ULTRA Z

We had the opportunity to drive the Ultra Z at the General Motors Proving Grounds in Milford, Michigan. It was quite an experience for anyone who loves Z28s.

Fig. 7-12. Both hood and fender louvers are functional. They exhaust hot underhood air.

156

Fig. 7-13. The Ultra Z callout on the side makes sure everyone knows what it is.

Handlingwise, the car felt like a really good handling Z28. There frankly wasn't much difference between a stock Z and the Ultra Z. But we could feel a slightly sharper response, a little more bite in corners, and we knew we could take favorite turns two or

Fig. 7-14. The wheels are experimental 8-inch wide versions of stock '80 spoked wheel. Tires are experimental P-metric 60-series steel-belted radials.

three miles per hour faster. There is no question that the fatter 60-series radials helped the Z's over-the-road performance.

But like we said before, the real story was under the hood. So we spent as much time as possible blasting up through the gears on acceleration runs. Driving a fuel-injected, turbocharged car is not like driving a big inch musclecar. You don't have gobs of sheer

Fig. 7-15. Rear ¾ view of the Ultra Z, showing an add-on rear deck spoiler.

torque melting the rear tires as you fishtail off the line. You aren't pinned back into your seat with compressed eyeballs from rpm one.

Instead, you nail the throttle and you steer the car as the revs and speed build up almost imperceptively at first, then faster and faster, in a giant rush forward. Just a slow, long, steady pressure that builds and builds rather than a dump-the-clutch blast that rams your spine into the back seat.

The Ultra Z was smooth and fast. We easily topped 120 mph on the speedometer before one of the proving ground security and safety people called a halt to my top speed runs. Meanwhile, we had clicked off a brace of zero-to-60 runs that averaged about 6.5 seconds. That's quick for a 3600 pound car with a 3.42 gear. Since we didn't have access to a marked-off quarter mile, we couldn't time the car on a dragstrip run. But we'd estimate that the car could click off the quarter in 14.9 seconds at 98-100 mph. And that's 1968 Z28 performance levels!

Although this is being written in the summer of 1979, we have it on good authority that Chevrolet will offer a special Z28 that incorporates many of the design features of the Ultra Z.

We know that Chevrolet will offer a turbocharged engine option in the Z. But it won't be the fuel-injected aluminum 350 in the Ultra Z. Instead, it will probably be the 301 4-barrel (4.9 liter) Pontiac engine offered as an option in the 1980 Pontiac Trans-Am.

As part of the package, buyers will probably get the unique deck lid spoiler, steering wheel and wheel/tire combination of the Ultra Z.

So if you stop for a light and you see a whale-tail mean and nasty Z28 pull up next to you, I wouldn't try it if I were you.

Index